CW01506430

PORTRAITS OF THE INSANE
The Case of Dr Diamond

PORTRAITS OF THE INSANE
The Case of Dr Diamond

Adrienne Burrows & Iwan Schumacher

Quartet Books
London New York

First published in English by Quartet Books Ltd 1990
A member of the Namara Group
27/29 Goodge Street, London W1P 1FD

Copyright © by Syndikat Autoren-und
Verlagsgesellschaft, Frankfurt am Main, 1979
Illustrations and Plates copyright © by their
various holding institutions 1990

First published in German in a translation by
Udo Rennert
by Syndikat Autoren-und Verlagsgesellschaft
1979 Frankfurt am Main as
Doktor Diamonds Bildnisse Von Geisteskranken

British Library Cataloguing in Publication Data
Burrows, Adrienne
Portraits of the insane: the case of Doctor Diamond
1. Mentally ill——Germany——History——
19th century
I. Title   II. Schumacher, Iwan   III. Doctor
Diamonds Bildnisse von Geisteskranken. *English*
362.2′0943   RA78   RA790.7.G3

ISBN 0-7043-2614-0

Typeset by AKM Associates (UK) Ltd, Southall
Printed and bound in Great Britain by
BPCC Hazell Books Aylesbury, Bucks

Contents

Preface

When this book was first published in 1979 we left open the question of the attribution of the photographs in the archives of the Royal Bethlem Hospital. Thought at that time probably to be prints by a photographer, Henry Hering, from Diamond's originals, these photographs are now considered to be the work of Hering, about whom little else is still known.

As no other major discoveries have been made in this field in the last fifteen years to enable us to change or broaden our account of these portraits significantly, we have left the main body of the text much as it was, with Diamond as its focusing point – a position he occupied in the 1850s in all matters concerning the application of photography to the study of mental disorder.

Acknowledgements

Grateful thanks to the very many people who answered our queries, offered information and granted access to libraries and archives, among them Carolyn Bloore, Gail Buckland, Morton N. Cohen, Joe Coltharp, E.H. Cornelius, Eric J. Freeman, K.J. Garlick, Philip Hepworth, Jean M. Kennedy, Leonard Pierce, N.H. Robinson, Robert A. Sobieszek, U. Terry, F.H. Thompson, Philip Wade, Alexander Walk, with special thanks to Patricia Allderidge at the Bethlem archives and Ian Lodge Patch at Springfield Hospital.

The information and guidance given by Erwin H. Ackerknecht, Richard Hunter and R.D. Laing have proved invaluable, so too the advice and encouragement of Geoffrey Barker, Ian Kennedy, Dave Solomon, Katrin Trümpy and Valerie Lloyd.

In the production of this book we are greatly indebted to Horst Kolo for re-photographing the photographs, to Tony Mathews and Barry Miller, to Reinhard Kaiser, Karl Markus Michel, Axel Rütters and Irmela Rütters at Syndikat.

Dr Diamond's paper 'On the Application of Photography to the Physiognomic and Mental Phenomena of Insanity' is reproduced by kind permission of the President and Council of the Royal Society.

The publishers would like to thank all the following institutions for permission to use their material:

Illustrations in the text

International Museum of Photography, Rochester, NY
Norwich Central Library, Norwich
Ashmolean Museum, Oxford
Royal Institution, London
Society of Antiquaries, London
Norfolk Record Office, Norwich
Royal Photographic Society, Bath
Westhill Library, Wandsworth, London
The Bethlem Royal Hospital, Archives, Beckenham, Kent
Royal Society of Medicine, London

Plates

Plates 1–16: Royal Society of Medicine, London
Plate 17: Royal College of Surgeons, London
Plates 18–20: Royal Society of Medicine, London
Plate 21: Royal Photographic Society, Bath.
Plates 22–71: The Bethlem Royal Hospital, Beckenham, Kent

Illustrations in the Text

Introduction

We are surrounded by things which have been lost – some have simply disappeared, others have gone unnoticed and so appear not to exist. It is after all quite possible to look at something without seeing it, and rediscovery, however much it seems like prising something out of nothing, usually comes from a change in perspective. What you find was there already but had become invisible.

We first heard of Dr Diamond in 1972 at the Victoria and Albert Museum's exhibition of Victorian photography – not an exhibition which promised many surprises.[1] It seemed to be the natural outcome of much well-publicized research into the work of early photographers (Hill and Adamson, Fox Talbot, Daguerre, Nadar, Fenton, Cameron, Carroll, etc.), and came at the height of a fashion for Victoriana, for the nostalgia of family albums and sepia prints. The work of the early masters was comparatively well known, and the average Victorian photograph had become something of a visual cliché. The very title of the exhibition, a comment made by Lady Eastlake, wife of the Director of the National Gallery back in the 1850s, seemed designed to set the photographs at a distance – 'From today painting is dead'. Who would deny that the lady had been wrong? – and emphasizing such an error, however interesting, only underlined the gulf in time between us and the photographs. So we went to the exhibition quite unprepared for the impact one group of six portraits was to make.[2]

Even now it is impossible to analyse their effect – except to say that these portraits did not look Victorian. They had a directness, an immediacy – they defied history. A woman in checked dress sat, smiling, holding a pigeon in her lap; a pale old man looked sideways into the distance; another woman, hands held together, lips apart, looked straight out at us. The looks they gave cut across differences of time and place with an energy of expression, a sense of the actual liveliness, however exhausted or depleted, inhabiting the human frame. Obviously they were not fashion-plate Victorians, neither could they be categorized to illustrate the conditions of a social class, despite their apparent poverty. The very creases in their clothes made their costume a part only of themselves. Portrayed in the quiet anonymity of the studio, everything about them contributed to a sense of timelessness. The photographs were by Dr Diamond. The people he portrayed were all mental patients.

For months afterwards these photographs remained fixed in the memory – prompting questions. Who was Dr Diamond? Where was the main body of his work? As a psychiatrist in a public asylum he had photographed his patients – little more was known. The six prints exhibited came from an album in the Royal Sociey of Medicine – a project begun by several members in 1862 but abandoned soon afterwards.[3] Diamond had contributed two dozen portraits with case-notes, but the case-books had since been lost. One other photograph of a patient had survived in good condition in an album in the Royal Photographic Society, together with a handful of hopelessly faded loose prints.

Repeatedly we were told that no more existed, yet they looked like a part of a much larger series. The conviction that he must have taken

1

more, the idea that finding more would tell more about Diamond, finally made us begin to look for them.

It was then that we found a series of articles by Dr John Conolly, published in 1858 in the *Medical Times and Gazette* and illustrated with engravings, 'from photographs by Dr Diamond' – tantalizing suggestions of lost originals.[4] More than this, Conolly described individual cases – who they were, where they came from, how they were treated in the asylums – so introducing us to the patients portrayed and giving a glimpse of Dr Diamond's work as a psychiatrist. (We have included these case-notes in this book, see below, p. 135.)

Conolly dispelled any doubts we had about the psychiatric validity of Diamond's photographic work for his contemporaries. He presented the portraits as an invaluable innovation and used them as Diamond himself had: to trace parallels between the patient's appearance and their mental states, a study they called 'The Physiognomy of Insanity'. He saw the photographs as Diamond's contribution to a new school of psychiatry practised in asylums throughout Britain in the 1850s – a school of reform based on the humane and scientific principles which, in the previous decades of the nineteenth century, had inspired a campaign for the total abolition of all forms of mechanical restraint (the irons, chains, straitjackets, etc., previously thought indispensable in the treatment of the insane). Fundamental to these reforms had been a change in attitude out of which the concept of the *mental patient* had come to replace that of the *lunatic* – a change which marked the beginnings of psychiatry as we know it today.

The old system placed all violent or troublesome patients in the position of dangerous animals. The new system regards them as afflicted persons, whose brain and nerves are diseased, and who are to be restored to health, and comfort, and reason. This simple difference of view it is which influences every particular in the arrangement of every part of an asylum for the insane.

Thus, whilst in the old asylums every arrangement was principally made for security and control, in the new, every arrangement is made for the cure of the malady, or the comfort of the insane.[5]

Our surprise, that so early in the nineteenth century a school of psychiatry should have sprung out of humanitarian principles and taken so humane a form, was in itself a revelation. It confirmed our unconscious reaction to the photographs and contradicted all our assumptions about Victorian psychiatry. This in turn gave a new dimension and fresh impetus to the research.

Discovering more about this period in psychiatry, it promised to be a comparatively simple task to find more photographs. They had been made by a psychiatrist as case records and research material at a time when psychiatry was attempting to bring its work within a scientific framework and win recognition as a valid branch of medicine. The data of asylum life were being recorded systematically for the first time and by forming societies and publishing their findings psychiatrists were making their work accessible to their contemporaries and safe for posterity. Much of this material has survived where it was deposited – but this did not seem to be the case with Diamond's photographs.

At Springfield Hospital, the former Surrey County Lunatic Asylum, where Diamond lived and worked in the 1850s, we found that though the case-books of Diamond's colleague, Mr Snape, had survived, Diamond's had disappeared. The asylum's annual reports, while telling of the introduction of a choir, a band and a pigeon house for the patients by Mr Snape, made no mention of Dr Diamond's photography. There were no photographs – nor anything to suggest that any had ever been made or kept there.

Looking further afield in the collections of various medical and scientific institutions proved equally unsuccessful until, one day, opening a brown paper parcel in the archives of the Bethlem Royal Hospital, we found ourselves face to face with four portraits already familiar from the illustrations to Conolly's articles, part of a series of more than fifty probably made as a private collection for Sir Charles Hood, who had held the post of Medical Superintendent at Bethlem in the 1850s. There were no case-notes with these photographs other than simple classifications of the patients' conditions written with their initials under the portraits. They were documented only as the former property of Hood.[6]

1

Still life, 1855 (*Diamond*)

To complicate the issue further, what were we to make of the fact that on some of the mounts, there was a credit 'Hering photo'? The *Medical Times and Gazette* had ascribed one of these portraits to Diamond. The series looked like the work of one photographer. Had Hering simply supplied a set of prints from Diamond's originals?[7]

Only one thing was certain – that for all this sudden wealth of portraiture we knew little more about Dr Diamond and his work. But the fact that we had found no more portraits of Diamond's own patients, that apparently he had not deposited them officially in any institution, did suggest that they had meant more to him than just records of his cases. After all, one has only to look at the portraits to see it is too simple merely to classify them as 'medical records', to name Dr Diamond 'Britain's first medical photographer', and let it go at that.

So who was this Dr Diamond? Today the answer is still incomplete, as is the collection of portraits presented in this book. What we found of him – the circles he moved in, the more public side of his private life – did lead to various photographs scattered through the collections of his friends and fellow members of antiquarian and photographic societies. Wherever we were able to trace photographs the link with Diamond had been social rather than professional.

In his later years especially, Dr Diamond preferred to appear in public as an amateur photographer and antiquarian, as a connoisseur who gave good dinners, rather than as a psychiatrist. The reputation which lasted all his life was made in the society rooms and dining clubs of the London of Thackeray and Douglas Jerrold. On his death in 1886 it was the *Athenaeum*, not the medical journals, which paid

3

a lengthy tribute full of anecdotes of Diamond and his antiquarian collections:

> It would be easier to name the kinds of things which Diamond never collected, than to produce a perfect list of those he did at some time or other.[8]

The fact that his museum of a home, Twickenham House, also served as the private asylum from which he made his living for the last thirty years of his life was thought scarcely worth mentioning, while the opportunity to assess Diamond's career in psychiatry was sidestepped, with a trick of rhetoric:

> From its outset to its close, Diamond's professional career was alike honourable to himself and beneficial to others; but one must look away from his medical record for the causes of the high regard in which he was held.

The tone adopted by the *Athenaeum* might not have seemed so obviously evasive had we not already heard something of one story which it did not mention. Earlier in this research our request to search Springfield Hospital Archives had been referred to a consultant on the staff who just then was preparing an article for publication on Diamond's colleague Mr Snape.[9] Central to his study was an event which occurred at the hospital in 1856: the death of a patient, Daniel Dolley, while under Mr Snape's care. From the story he told us it was clear that although the subsequent official enquiries were concerned with Mr Snape's handling of the case, Dr Diamond had become involved, and the final outcome had precipitated his resignation from the asylum in 1858.

To find out more about Diamond's part we looked up a parliamentary report on the proceedings in the library of the House of Lords.[10] Reading the evidence – the statements given by Snape, Diamond and the attendents on the ward, the opinions of contemporary psychiatrists, and the account of the reactions and subsequent actions both of the asylum's local managing committee and of the national body responsible for overseeing asylum affairs, the Commissioners in Lunacy, we realized that we had found far more than just an explanation for Diamond's resignation. Instead of photographs we had found a story which in some strange way amounted to their narrative counterpart.

This story, like the photographs, is essentially timeless. True it evolves within a wealth of precise, often picturesque historical detail, starting from the day that Dolley died on what was meant to be Mr Snape's morning off – 'his horse and carriage waiting below to take him to the Crystal Palace'. And it is equally true that it tells a great deal about a particular phase in psychiatry – the attitudes of psychiatrists to their patients, their opinions of various forms of treatment, etc. – when Diamond was taking his photographs. But the conflicts at its centre, the irony inherent in its outcome, these are by no means unique to the mid-nineteenth century. The story begins with the death of a patient. It progresses through incidents bizarre, pathetic, ridiculous, even macabre, in their details, to a point where Dolley's death is lost from sight as various people in various positions of power simply compete for the right to enforce their own interpretations on the chaos.

So it is not just for historical authenticity that we have told the case in much the same way as it unfolds in the parliamentary report, but because there is an inevitability in this story, something in the way these events move towards their conclusion which, seen in retrospect, forms an intriguing parallel to Diamond's portraits. Like the proverbial missing link it finally begins to account for their tragic aspect, their peculiarly powerful impact.

The part played by Diamond in this case is an extreme example of the general pattern of his life. Diamond had always moved in the mainstream of mid-Victorian intellectual and social life. He was conservative by nature, but this conservatism was constantly being challenged by his extraordinarily active curiosity, making him, though not himself an inventor or reformer, unusually receptive to the photographic inventions and psychiatric innovations of his more adventurous or tenacious colleagues.[11] Diamond was a man who in 1850 had found himself in the right place at the right time to emerge from that mainstream almost in spite of himself and make his startlingly original 'Portraits of the Insane'.[12]

Then the Snape Case had come. As the issues involved and Diamond's part in the case are dealt with in detail later on, it is enough to say that when, for reasons stunningly irrelevant to the central problems of the case, Diamond emerged in official disgrace, his reaction as always was to take things as they came. He resigned his post, and with it the opportunity to photograph his patients, set up a small private asylum in Twickenham, and immersed himself in antiquarianism and the technicalities of photography for the last thirty years of his life. His photographs went with him – one more of the many collections 'more curious than valuable' which were the by-products of a singular life.

And what did Diamond do with his photographs? Unlike many of his contemporaries he had never treated them as independent works of art. For him photography had been supremely useful – had the photographs then outlived their usefulness? Whatever his reason, the man who had devoted so much of his life to collecting curiosities saw death as the time to disperse them all again. When Diamond died in 1886, he left instructions in his will to sell Twickenham House and all its contents, the proceeds to go to his daughter. A catalogue of the sale has been preserved in Twickenham Public Library showing that among the items auctioned were Diamond's photographic equipment and albums.[13] No record was kept of where any items went – and we have not been able to find them.

So in many ways this book is a record of an uneasy compromise – the terms dictated by Diamond himself. Many of our questions have been answered so that we have been able to assemble biographical information to show something of how and why Diamond came to make these portraits, and how his contemporaries reacted to them; we have looked at the conditions under which they were made in the early years of the asylum era in psychiatry, through an account of the Snape Case. Finally we have examined the ways in which Diamond's personal photographic study of the physiognomy of insanity fitted into current psychiatric theory and practice.

Much more remains – but here the photographs must speak for themselves. 'The photographer,' as Diamond once said, 'needs in many cases no aid from any language of his own, but prefers rather to listen, with the picture before him, to the silent but telling language of nature'.[14]

1
Dr Hugh Welch Diamond

It is not surprising that Diamond became a psychiatrist – his father was a mad-house keeper. In 1820, when Hugh, the eldest child, was only twelve years old, his father, William Bachelor Diamond, closed his general practice in Sussex, moved his family to London and opened a private asylum in St Pancras.[1] The Diamond family lived on the premises, as was the usual practice, and so brought their son into close contact with mental patients – a way of life which Diamond himself was to take up professionally before his father retired and which he later saw continued by his own eldest son.[2] The family connection with the mad-house business spanned ninety years: Diamond was involved for almost sixty-five.

William Bachelor Diamond was a tough, resilient man – qualities much in demand in psychiatric practice at a time when the daily management of the insane usually amounted to little more than constant physical coercion. He had begun his medical career at sea, as a surgeon's mate in the East India Company, amid the perils of enemy attacks, storms and epidemics, and gained his promotion to the rank of surgeon through the death of his predecessor in India. Considering these working conditions, the pay was poor – the compensation being that surgeons were allowed to trade on their own account, so that many of those who survived made considerable fortunes.[3]

Each voyage lasted for nearly two years. Within weeks of returning from his first voyage William Bachelor married Jane Welch, who came from a village close to his own house in Brenchley, Kent, setting sail for India again

2
Dr Diamond, Self-portrait, 1850s

only three months later – by which time his wife was expecting their first child.[4] Hugh Welch Diamond was born in Goudhurst, Kent on 23 October 1808, while his father was still at sea.

William Bachelor settled in England as a general practitioner in the early years of the Regency. The case of George III's madness had erupted suddenly twenty years earlier on a society where insanity, hardly even thought of as disease and with correspondingly small hope of cure, had previously condemned the sufferer to the status of prisoner or outcast. For the King to be mad was almost inconceivable. Certainly it brought the question of insanity out of its former obscurity, making it a subject of debate in Parliament, and throughout society.[5] It is hardly surprising that the private mad-house business flourished and that psychiatry increasingly attracted the interest of physicians for a variety of scientific, humanitarian and financial reasons. William Bachelor Diamond opened his asylum in the year the mad King died.[6]

The family was not wealthy, though well connected in Kent and claiming descendancy from the old Huguenot family, Demonte.[7] Only months after opening his asylum William Bachelor found it financially necessary to make one more trip to India. Soon afterwards when Hugh Diamond began his medical apprenticeship he had to find employment in a private practice to cover the cost of his formal studies. He served his five-year apprenticeship in his father's asylum rather than in general medical practice.

Diamond's training and early professional practice were typically those of a future Victorian: a mixture of private initiative and public service when the recipients in these two sectors were rigidly divided according to class. It was a time which saw a significant attempt at standardization in training, with a well-defined curriculum of compulsory lectures and hospital practice; a time when the social problems inherent in the process of industrialization had begun to make themselves apparent. Already attempts were being made to contain these problems by institutionalizing them within the social system.[8] Diamond was a medical student when the age of the workhouse, the public asylum and the hospital was in its infancy, and when the problems of housing, sanitation and hygiene of an overworked, overcrowded urban pauper population were beginning to emerge as crucial issues of industrialized society.

As soon as Diamond qualified, family influence helped him to his first job. His cousin, Thomas Charles, was a governor of the new Dispensary in Maidstone and one of its voluntary physicians was a Dr Welch, a relation of his mother. The Dispensary, set up by Maidstone's more benevolent citizens, supported by charity and small fees from patients, opened in 1830 with Diamond in the administrative post of

Resident Apothecary at a salary of sixty pounds a year.[9] This was the sort of post from which a young physician could hope to build a career in hospital practice, but Diamond did not stay there long, and nine months later he was back in London, setting up his own private practice in the fashionable district of Soho Square.

Then came the cholera – from India across Asia to the Baltic, from Hamburg to Sunderland – and in February 1832, it broke out in London.

> Listen to the tales of the wretched poor (who are unfortunately the class of person generally attacked with cholera) and you will hear, that in times of sickness and distress, none except medical gentlemen enter their miserable abodes, hear the cries of their starving children, or feel the chill produced by their cold and damp apartments. The general practitioners of London have volunteered their services to attend cholera patients, and furnish medicines gratuitously. Parishes have their medical boards, and convene frequently for the benefit of the poor. Cholera hospitals are filled up under their superintendence; much valuable time must be consumed in these employments while their private practice and their family interests are neglected.[10]

This letter, written to *The Times* by a physician on the same parish board of health as Diamond, calls upon the 'wretched poor' as witnesses to the zeal of general practitioners rather than their effectiveness. Such a defence reflects something of the panic to which cholera gave rise in medical circles. In the first seven weeks 1,500 cases occurred in London – half of them fatal, and when the epidemic finally died out medical opinion remained as confused as ever about the nature of the disease, its cause and cure. The improvised health system was soon abandoned, and Diamond, like most other physicians who attended the poor during the outbreak, returned to private practice. Cholera in Diamond's case had amounted to a final testing-ground. When little more than a student he had been confronted with one of the worst epidemics the country had ever known, over which there seemed to be little medical control. As a physician he had gone in against it with his fellows, done what he could – and had had the good fortune to survive. He remembered this time all his life with a degree of pride.

Diamond stayed in private practice in London for eighteen years, until his appointment as a

Medical Superintendent of the Surrey County Asylum in 1849. Applying for this post he could claim twenty-five years experience of the management and treatment of the insane from his contact with his father's asylum. He had visited the old public asylum, Bethlem, for informal instruction from two of its physicians, Sir James Tuthill and Dr Edward Monroe, and although few formal qualifications were required for physicians to practise in asylums he had obtained a medical doctorate. Following a practice fairly common among medical students at that time, he had finished his studies 'on the continent', but proved exceptional in choosing to go to Kiel, Denmark. 'I am,' he stated at a later date, 'the only person in this country who possesses that degree, I believe. I think it a very honourable degree.' He had probably already decided to make a career in psychiatry while studying for it. 'I obtained it,' he said, 'after writing a thesis on insanity.'[11] Unfortunately, no trace of Diamond's degree, nor of his thesis can now be found at Kiel. All we know about Diamond's doctorate is that when he first applied for the post at the Surrey Asylum in 1848, his title was still Mr Diamond – and the post was given to a Mr Snape. When the second post of Medical Superintendent became vacant the following year, Diamond's application was successful, and he took up his new job as Dr Diamond.

In many ways the Dr Diamond who by 1850 found himself in charge of 400 pauper patients in one of England's new public asylums was unusually well qualified, both practically and theoretically, for the job. Much of the work involved was already familiar to him, which goes some way to explain the speed with which he began to make innovations of his own. What was new was the scale of operations – compared to the handful of patients in a private madhouse, in a public asylum it was possible to make simultaneous comparison of hundreds of cases. This was the situation in which, only months after taking up his post, Diamond began to make his photographic study of the physiognomies of the patients in his care.

What still requires some explanation is how Diamond had come to be a photographer, and

why he first came to use photography in his work.

In 1839, ten years before Diamond began work at the Surrey Asylum, the invention of photography was announced to the public. The physicist Arago reported the success of Daguerre's experiments to the Académie des Sciences on 7 January. Three weeks later, William Henry Fox Talbot, who had been working independently on a different method,

3
Hugh W. Diamond, 1839 (*from a drawing by I. Archer*)

rushed into publication with his paper 'Some Account of the Art of Photogenic Drawing', and within weeks his working methods and materials were made available commercially.

In April, three months after Talbot's announcement, Diamond purchased some photogenic drawing-paper and made his first

4
Rev. Joseph Bancroft Reade, *c.* 1855 (*Diamond*)

photograph – a contact print of a pattern of lace.[12] His immediate response to the invention was to find out for himself how it worked. Before finding any use for photography he set himself to master its technicalities, to learn to operate them with his own hands. In this he displayed his independence as a researcher – unwilling simply to accept from others what he could work out for himself, he was quite prepared, whenever necessary, to play the part of the technician. It would have been altogether out of character had Diamond the psychiatrist later thought up his photographic project at the Surrey Asylum and then commissioned a photographer to carry it out for him. His 'Portraits of the Insane' were to be the product of his outstanding technical competence – the skill coming first.

Diamond's early photographic activities were concerned with the technical problems of Talbot's process. He was one of a minority at that time who, when comparing the two photographic processes, was not dazzled by the superior brilliance and detail of the Daguerreo-

type. His very first introduction to photography had been watching the experiments of his astronomer friend from the Numismatic Society, the Rev J.B. Reade, one of a handful of scientists who recognized the potential of Talbot's process – that as a negative/positive process it produced multiple prints and that this could be of considerable use in their own fields – and had begun their own research to improve the quality of the Talbotype.[13] Quite apart from difficulties in the actual manipulation (true of both processes), with the Talbotype no amount of manual dexterity could yet overcome the lack of clarity and detail in the prints produced. This process was still a subject for research and for many years Diamond made few photographs other than for experimental purposes.

Photography for him was an extension of an interest in technology which had previously found its focusing-point in his antiquarian researches. He studied history principally through artefacts and inventions, acquiring his collections not so much for their intrinsic value as for evidence in his investigations into the

9

process used in their production – how it worked, when it had been invented and by whom. Several years before his first experiments with photography, Diamond had assembled one of the finest collections of early mezzotint engravings in the country in order to study the origins of the process and in his first paper to the Society of Antiquaries he had reattributed the invention, claimed by Prince Rupert, to Louis von Siegen.[14] He sold his collection to the British Museum once he had made his point. On another occasion, a colleague gave him an Egyptian mummy found at a Custom House sale. Diamond not only examined it in the context of his previous researches into Egyptian antiquities, which enabled him to date it – he also saw it as an extension of his own experiments in mummification by the process of drying. Finding a similarity of method he wrote to the Society of Antiquaries:

5
Cavalier's Glove,
1853 (*Diamond*)

> I take the liberty of sending you a small hand of an infant which I treated so myself eighteen years since; it has been constantly exposed to the atmosphere and no doubt, if wrapped in bandages and protected from the air, would last as long as any Egyptian mummy which ever was made.[15]

In taking up the study of antiquities, Diamond had turned to a subject which, like medicine, was already well established in his family. His cousin Thomas Charles (already mentioned as a governor of the Maidstone Dispensary), who was thirty years older than Diamond and also a physician, was well known as an antiquarian collector. When Diamond was only beginning to build the collections which he later housed in Twickenham, Charles had already set up a private museum in his home, Chillington House. Charles was a man of sentiment – he translated Boethius, toured Britain's historic sites making sketches (on which he noted details of various ailments he suffered from while making them) and with a romantic taste for ruins built two in his garden – one in the Roman style and a second, as a memorial to his brother, in the Gothic, taking the design from the ruins of the chapel in the castle at Hastings. In his unorthodox methods of reconstruction he apparently committed such offence against the taste of the following generation that his contemporaries had to defend him from absolute ridicule. One

archaeologist, recalling his Roman room, wrote:

> From examples I had sent him of Roman wall-paintings discovered in London, he had papered the room with coloured paper, so as to represent, with truthfulness and good effect, the interior of a Roman room in a house in Londinium. What if the room had sash windows? The general aspect of a Roman dwelling-room was secured, and that was all Mr Charles contemplated.[16]

Whatever conflicts arose over his museum, the exhibits he kept there earned him unqualified respect. His collection of rare fossils was admired by the Marquess of Northampton; two Indian gentlemen who visited Charles on their tour of Britain especially noted 'ancient coins, a quantity of old armour, and curiosities without number' – as well as a valuable Indian inlaid chest.[17] Pride of place in his collections belonged to the Roman antiquities which Charles had excavated himself from local Kent sites.

Charles was, in fact, extraordinarily like – yet unlike – the Dr Diamond who spent the last years of his life in Twickenham House. They met on a wide range of topics, and differed in approach. Charles was steeped in nostalgia for the poetry of the past. Diamond, in an age of scientific optimism, looked at the past with one eye on the future. True, for all his scientific rigour, he was still capable of momentary 'lapses' into a more sentimental vein. He delighted in the discovery that his garden fence at Twickenham had been built from swords collected on the battlefield at Culloden. And when he had convinced his fellow antiquarians of the value of photography as an objective method of recording in scientific investigations, he then presented their society with picturesque views of 'Shakespeare's Home' and 'Anne Hathaway's Cottage' as the results of a photographic tour of ancient buildings. But in general his various activities, regardless of topic, were part of a scientific search for the order of things. Typical of his motives and methods as a researcher is a story told by a friend about Diamond's collection of old wine bottles, brought out to answer a query at a Twickenham dinner party:

> Soon the table was covered with black bottles, and Diamond gave a brief lecture on their peculiarities. It would have delighted Darwin, for it showed how the bottle had relinquished its original globular form at an early date in the eighteenth century, and subsequently assumed each of its successive shapes in order to adapt itself to the new conditions imposed on creatures of its particular kind by new fashions of cellaring and storing bottled wine.[18]

The logical progression had been revealed quite rationally – simply by acquiring *all* the evidence. 'My set of old wine bottles,' said Diamond, 'is perfect.'

It was this search for completeness which directed Diamond in his researches, making him truly a collector – as much of mental patients as of antiquities.

In the 1840s, while Diamond was in general practice, one of his patients was a sculptor, Frederick Scott Archer. A friendship grew up between the two men, a collaboration of mutual interests, which was to give a fresh impetus to Diamond's work as a photographer. Archer's invention of the wet-collodion process in 1850 led directly to Diamond's 'Portraits of the Insane'.

For all his intellectual independence, very few of Diamond's activities were carried out in isolation. He thrived on intellectual contacts, on the stimulus of other people's ideas and the exchange of specialist knowledge, and his colleagues played an active part in Diamond's

6
Interior of the Abbey, Edinburgh, 1854 (*Diamond*)

7
Shakespeare's Home, 1854 (*Diamond*)

8
Anne Hathaway's Cottage, Shotterley, 1854 (*Diamond*)

11

researches through a network of London clubs and societies. As an antiquarian Diamond remained active all his life as a Fellow of the Society of Antiquaries and a member of the Numismatic Society. As a psychiatrist he joined the Association of Medical Officers of Asylums and Hospitals for the Insane, was elected Honorary Secretary in 1852, and as a photographer he was a founder member of the Photographic Society and was elected Secretary and Editor of its journal in 1859. This is the context in which Diamond's friendship with Archer flourished.

It began when Archer, looking for a cheap way to catalogue his sculptures, asked Diamond to teach him the Calotype process (the name given by Talbot to his invention when he took out a patent in 1842), and in 1847 both men joined a group of colleagues to set up the Calotype Club – a photographic society 'for the exchange of information from which improvements might result'. Archer, sharing his colleagues' dissatisfaction with the quality of Calotype prints, was extraordinary for the single-mindedness with which he set himself to improve it. Photography soon became something of an obsession at the expense of his career as a sculptor.

As a member of the Calotype Club, Diamond was as diverse in his activities as ever. In 1847 he was elected a Fellow of the Royal Institution, proposed by its President, Michael Faraday; he organized a dig at Ewell, Surrey, retrieving five cartloads of Roman pottery and other funeral remains, and taking Archer along to make drawings as records of their finds; and he was about to embark on his new career in psychiatry.[19]

By the time Diamond was appointed Medical Superintendent of Female Patients at the Surrey Asylum, Archer had begun his experiments to find an alternative medium to paper for the photographic negative, and soon after Diamond and his family took up residence at the asylum in Wandsworth,[20] Archer summoned him for the first demonstration of his new photographic process.[21] This was the beginning of a new phase in photography, opening up possibilities for professionals and amateurs, which had previously been frustrated by technical deficiencies.

Diamond and Archer spent the day experimenting, taking photographs through a microscope of fossils, wood, infusioria, etc. – experiments reminiscent of Diamond's first photographic activities with the astronomer, Reade.[22]

Like the Calotype, Archer's was a negative/positive process, but instead of paper he used glass coated with a wet collodion for his negatives. Its sensitivity produced results to rival the Daguerreotype in brilliance of detail, and it reduced exposure time from minutes to seconds.

Diamond, recognizing the immense potential of his friend's invention, lost no time in setting up a photographic studio of his own. And since

9
Mrs Diamond, Dr Diamond's second wife, 1850s (*Diamond*)

he had just moved to the Surrey Asylum, that is where he set up his studio.

For all its improvements over previous methods, the collodion process still involved a series of delicate operations. To make a successful photograph required practice. Archer had become so involved with the invention itself that he no longer had any particular interest in using it. As long as improvements were needed,

10

Dr Diamond and friends at Springfield Asylum: Diamond (with dog), Philip Delamotte (third from left),
J.J. Forrester (seated), 1850s (*Count de Montizon*)

requiring further research, he was reluctant to spend time acquiring skill as a photographer.

Diamond went straight for the skill. He mastered the collodion in order to make photographs – and he mastered it by making photographs, practising photography in the variety of circumstances offered by his other interests. When Archer suggested a camera in which the wet-plates could also be developed, Diamond worked at outdoor photography as an antiquarian photographing historic buildings. In his studio he photographed manuscripts, engravings and various antiquarian objects. And he made portraits – of his friends, his family and his patients. Diamond's portraits of his patients were the product of two interests, one of which happened to be his job; and the circumstances of his job, living at the asylum with patients always available to be photographed, made it comparatively easy to combine the two. It would, in fact, have been extraordinary had Diamond *not* made his 'Portraits of the Insane'.

At first these portraits did not occupy any special place in Diamond's photographic output – not until the exhibitions of the 1850s were they seen in public – and by then he had already emerged as one of the leading photographers of his day, not for any particular group of photographs but because of his technical skill.

The comparative simplicity of the collodion process tempted many amateurs to take up photography, led by the antiquarians who, before any photographic journal existed, asked the Editor of *Notes & Queries* to publish a simple account of how to take photographs.[23] Diamond, himself an antiquarian and one of the most experienced practitioners of the new process, was an obvious choice as author, and in September 1852, his articles begin to appear in *Notes & Queries* – the first popular photographic manual ever published.

'I wish it to be understood,' he cautioned his readers, 'that I may offer but little that is original, my object being to describe, as plainly as I possibly can, these easy methods.'[24] What he offered was experience, seen in his promise 'to make no observation but what I have found to be successful in my own hands'. Diamond proved immensely popular as a teacher. He

explained the various operations in a way which made them comprehensible even to complete beginners, alerting his readers to potential pitfalls and adding whatever practical hints he had worked out from his own experiences. He aimed to eliminate the mystique surrounding photography, which threatened to make it a specialist subject, by constantly emphasizing how easy it all was, given a little practice. And he published an open invitation to readers to bring their technical problems to him personally at the Surrey Asylum where he would attempt to clarify them by giving demonstrations – an invitation many photographers took up, including the young Lewis Carroll.[25]

These articles in *Notes & Queries* made Diamond's reputation. When the Photographic Society was set up in 1853 Diamond was made a council member and helped to organize exhibitions, a photographic exchange society, an antiquarian section and various groups for photographic outings. One photograph has survived of such a group posed at the front door of the Surrey Asylum.[26] When Diamond convinced the Society of Antiquaries of the need for an official photographer, the society duly bestowed the honour on Diamond.[27] He had, in fact, made a place for himself at the centre of the photographic world – a world which cut across the strata of society.

Queen Victoria and Prince Albert were keen photographers. Diamond had exhibited photographs at the Earl of Rosse's soirées, when the Earl was President of the Royal Society, and he had begun to make a series of photographs for publication of his 'Portraits of the Men of the Time'.[28] He photographed his friends, fellow members of Douglas Jerrold's 'Our Club' when Jerrold was Editor of *Punch*. He photographed his fellow photographers: Roger Fenton, Philip Delamotte, and the Count de Montizon. He photographed Dr Conolly, the psychiatrist, the meteorologist James Glaisher, who was also a photographer, Charles Vignoles, civil engineer and photographer, and the Rev. Reade, astronomer, photographer and Chaplain to the Buckinghamshire Asylum. These last four, appearing in their professional capacities, were later to give evidence in the Snape Case – showing how small, how tightly woven London

11
Dr Diamond and Thomas G. Mackinlay, 1850s

society then was. It was a social world which, once Diamond had gained access to it, soon came to acknowledge his success:

> The eminent services rendered by Dr Diamond to Photography and through Photography to Archaeology, have given rise to a general feeling that he is entitled to some public acknowledgement in the nature of a Testimonial. Scarcely any of the practicers of photography have not received great benefit from the suggestions and improvements of Dr Diamond. These improvements have been the results of numerous and costly experiments, carried on in the true spirit of scientific enquiry, and afterwards explained in the most frank and liberal manner: without the slightest reservation or endeavour to obtain from them any private or personal advantage.[29]

Socially Diamond was well situated. His friends – photographers, scientists and many other 'Men of the Time' subscribed to this testimonial and presented him with a purse of £300. He had indeed given his services to photography freely, a point to which the organizers of the testimonial gave great emphasis, for they were then engaged in a legal battle with

Fox Talbot to make him relinquish the last of his photographic patents.[30] But what of Archer? He had not patented his process, with which many photographers were then making fortunes, and he continued his photographic research with no financial reward whatever. Not until his death, in 1855, was a testimonial set up to honour the inventor of the collodion process whose work had left his family almost penniless. The response to this appeal was slower, and Archer's widow had also died by the time a small purse of £160 was presented to the orphaned family.

Diamond, meanwhile, had moved on – he was now known as a photographer of mental patients.

Diamond rarely spent time publicly analysing or evaluating his own work. In all his writings on photography he seldom discussed his own photographs. When he did it was to illustrate a technical point, or as an example of how useful photography itself could be in scientific studies. When he wrote in praise of its 'unerring accuracy', he was not specifying his

15

12
Douglas Jerrold, journalist, playwright and humourist,
taken a fortnight before his death, 1857 (*Diamond*)

13
William J. Thoms, Editor of *Notes & Queries*, c. 1856

14
Philip H. Delamotte examining Diamond's still life,
c. 1856 (*see Illustration 1*)

15
Charles Vignoles, civil engineer, 1856 (*Diamond*)

own work, nor was he differentiating between photography's various applications.[31] His underlying implication was that all photographs, if technically competent, could be useful and were much the same. This not only implied a stylistic anonymity in his own case, but also that his photographs were of equal value whether of anitquarian or psychiatric subjects.

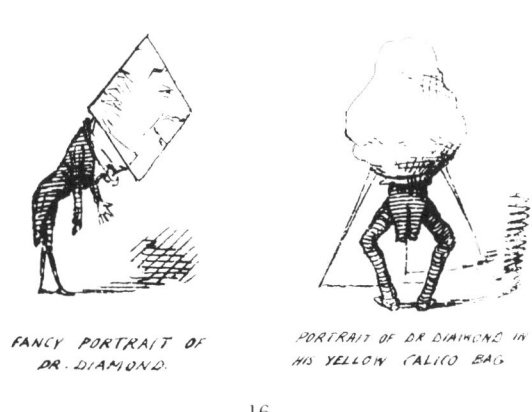

FANCY PORTRAIT OF DR. DIAMOND.

PORTRAIT OF DR DIAMOND IN HIS YELLOW CALICO BAG

16
Caricatures of Dr Diamond, 1855

Although theoretically admitting to no personal preferences, when it came to exhibiting his photographs, Diamond had to select. In 1852 the Society of Arts organized the first public exhibition entirely devoted to photographs. More than a thousand were on show – the work of the leading photographers of the day, and the exhibition was to be visited by the Queen and Prince Albert. Given the opportunity to reach a wider public than his immediate circle of friends and acquaintances, when it came to the general public who, encouraged by the critics, were to visit the exhibition in their thousands, Diamond chose to exhibit two sets of portraits labelled 'Types of Insanity'. Though they had been made for scientific study, he did not intend to keep them for specialist viewers.

The critics were too perplexed trying to construct a concept of photography to take much notice of individual exhibits. All photographs were remarkable. The very fact that they existed was seen as 'one of those marvellous results equally astonishing to the philosopher and the simple child'.[32] For the critics the invention itself was on display more than any of its products, and the photographers' work was usually described according to the process used

and the comparative level of technical skill. Looking at Diamond's portraits of his patients they saw 'a remarkable collection of positive pictures on glass'[33] – an example of the advances made since the invention of the wet-collodion process, 'by which the Doctor has been enabled to produce a group of portraits of insane and idiotic people who could probably not be induced to remain quiet long enough to be taken by the other processes'.[34]

Diamond was exhibiting the first photographs made for the study of insanity (which were also the first medical photographs made in this country),[35] but the process which made such ventures practicable was itself so new that most examples of applied photography exhibited were first in their respective fields:

The photographs of animals in the Zoological Gardens, Regents Park . . . executed by an amateur (Count de Montizon), are also highly interesting in both a popular and a scientific view. The Giraffe, the Hippopotamus, and especially the Polar Bear, are admirably represented. One of the pictures represents a fish swimming in a glass fern case: being probably the first actual portrait that was ever executed of a fish in its native element.[36]

Diamond's portraits of his patients apparently had more in common with the Count de Montizon's fish than with the numerous portraits exhibited of 'Ladies' and 'Gentlemen' – which at least meant that Diamond was exempt from the criticisms levelled at other portrait photographers. For many critics portraiture was a genre in which the scientific virtues of accuracy and truthfulness were unpalatable. One wrote:

Photographic and Daguerrotype portraits are often wanting in vivacity, individuality and beauty, bearing but little resemblance to the sitter, who recoils from the libel upon his personal appearance, none the more satisfied on being informed of the infallibility of Nature, who *never* flatters; but, I would ask, does Nature do justice?[37]

Portraiture, with its own traditions of patronage, had for centuries been the province of painters. Photography not only disturbed established perceptions of 'nature as viewed with the two eyes' – it also offered unwelcome competition.[38] Portraits of lunatics, outside any traditions of patronage and taste, were acceptable as scientific documents. And as such they were widely acclaimed the following year when the newly formed Photographic Society held its first exhibition.

As enthusiastic as ever, the critics noted that the standardization of processes was ridding photography of its 'glorious uncertainty', and

is destined to afford to our craft; to say nothing of the stone for stone representations of all the chief edifices in all parts of the world . . .[41]

The same criteria were used for Diamond's portraits. They were seen as a collection, without any reference to individual portraits, as a series

17a
Acute Puerperal Mania, 1850s (*Diamond*)

17b
The same patient, convalescent (*Diamond*)

this new technical competence, making photographs less 'mechanical', allowed photographers to produce 'varied results peculiar to themselves and unattainable by others – although using precisely the same means'.[39] It was in the eyes of the critics the great exhibition of applied photography, and in this context they stretched their vocabularies to include the 'niceties of taste'. Studies of animals, rock formations, architectural views, microscopic images, reproductions of chalk drawings and engravings – such photographs were 'beautiful', when beautiful was synonymous with 'useful'.[40] Photography was to be the great educator, and as such sheer quantity became a virtue:

> To the architect and civil engineer we commend a consideration of Mr Fenton's view of the progress of the bridge now constructing across the Dnieper; and to Mr Delamotte's views of the works of the Crystal Palace at Sydenham, as instances of the valuable aid photography

deserving praise precisely because their existence implied a use. The *Athenaeum* called them 'one of the most interesting series of the exhibition' – their interest being that 'the illustration of such subjects is obviously one of the most important purposes to which the art can be applied'.

Still no comparison was made with other portraits – no one discussed them as portraits or looked at them as individual photographs until Ernest Lacan reviewed them for the French photographic journal *La Lumière*. He was the first critic who wrote that these pictures illustrated more than just a useful application of photography. His review reflects something of the impact the portraits had on him:

> Some of them are smiling, others seem to be dreaming, and all have something strange about their physiognomy; that is what strikes one at first glance. Studying them at length, one cannot but be moved: all these faces bear an expression at once bizarre and painful.[42]

18

Lacan looked at portraits and he saw *people* – he noticed what no other critic had dealt with directly: 'Let one word suffice,' he said, 'they are insane.'

Lacan's willingness to linger over individual portraits and record the variety of emotions produced in him by the patients' expressions, and his ability as a critic to describe his response to the photograph in detail, met with approval from Diamond. A friendship developed between the two men, in which Lacan played the part of apologist to Diamond's portraits. After the 1854 photographic exhibition Diamond kept Lacan in touch with his work, sending him prints of his latest photographs which Lacan reviewed at length in *La Lumière*. When Lacan published a collection of his photographic reviews in 1855 under the title *Esquisses Photographiques*, he devoted one section to Diamond in which he described his work in the context of a visit to the Surrey Asylum. He also took up the story of one particular patient whose portrait he had described in an earlier review and who had since made several suicide attempts:

> One day she had cut her throat, and still bore the scar; on another occasion she had thrown herself from one of the windows of the asylum, but caused herself only bruises; finally a few months ago, in spite of being kept under surveillance, she managed to procure herself a knife, and, in the presence of one of the cleaning women (who struggled bravely with her) she succeeded this time in inflicting such a deep wound on her throat that her life could not be saved. Dr Diamond wished to preserve the image of this corpse. And, indeed, this print provides ample material for study and reflection.[43]

When Diamond himself presented an account of his photographic work at the Surrey Asylum in a paper to the Royal Society, he included an account of this case and exhibited both portraits. His account was given entirely through the voice of Lacan. Quoting his articles in French as commentaries to the portraits, he refused to add any descriptive comments of his own. Diamond remained silent; Lacan's conclusions are the only conclusions he gave:

> Calm has spread over those features, formerly tormented by convulsions; her half-open eyes, her almost smiling mouth seem to express the satisfaction of a desire fulfilled. Is this a final symptom of the illness? Or does it rather express what the unfortunate creature must have felt as her reason returned in the supreme moment of deliverance from a life of misery and pain? Only science can give us the answer.

It is not surprising that Lacan, as the first critic to take account of Diamond's portraits outside the confines of applied photography, should be the first to raise the issue of whether or not they should be exhibited. Diamond himself never showed the death portrait at a public exhibition. Lacan's view was that he 'could not have exhibited this print, which inspires such horror in the observer'.[44] For the rest, Lacan praised the *courage* of the man who had reproduced 'the features of the unhappy women entrusted to his care' and who had done so 'in the interests of his profession and to promote the study of mental diseases'. Far from advocating any form of censorship Lacan saw a place for the portraits not just among specialists but in society at large: 'When one has in one's possession riches such as these, one should let the public benefit from them.'

But in the photographic world where Diamond could exhibit his portraits tastes were changing. The invention of the collodion process, followed by the removal of the last of Talbot's patent restrictions in the mid-1850s, resulted in a commercial boom in portrait photography. Studios flourished. In 1852 London had a dozen professional photographers; five years later there were more than 150. As had previously been the case with Daguerreotypists, many of them were miniature painters who, converted to the more efficient art, brought with them the skill of satisfying their sitters. Flattery was their way of making a living – retouching, even colouring, were essential for customers with strong preconceptions as to how they should be represented. Commerce went hand in hand with triviality and amateur documentary photographers like Diamond found it increasingly difficult to maintain their favour with the critics who, at the Photographic Exhibition of 1857, welcomed the arrival of the 'artist-photographer', introducing the criterion of imagination:

> We like a picture which has a preponderance of darkness in it . . . What light contains we know and can catalogue, but darkness makes us think and fancy, and leads us by a back door into eternity, which no picture's four sides ever yet was a front entrance to.[45]

Forgetting all his former praise of applied photography, the delighted critic now saw himself 'called upon to examine and pronounce upon photographs as he would upon a gallery of water-colour drawings', which might explain some of the disappointment expressed by one critic in his review of some portraits of 'Crimean Heroes' exhibited by the photographers Cundall and Howlett:

> If they would throw a little imagination into their pictures, they would be admirable. The stern gaze which faced the cannon's roar unflinchingly, the thick moustache and beard grizzled and matted with exposure to the wind and storm, the wrinkles imprinted by night-watches and trench-work are there; but the men look as though sitting for their likeness, not as though they might be summoned any minute to death or glory.[46]

Diamond's 'Portraits of the Insane' continued to attract praise, although his patients were as anonymous and unpoetic as these Crimean heroes. It was the subject of insanity which satisfied the critic's obsession with imagination:

> The deprivation of reason is such an awful physical mystery, that any comment upon it has interest, whether in Dr Diamond's photographs, Shakespeare's Lear, or Scott's Gallathy.[47]

Looking at his photographs, one critic was reminded of Kaulbach's painting 'The Mad-house', and another found them as perfect as Hogarth's studies of maniacs. Once again their documentary content was ignored, not this time under the heading of 'applied photography', but as *Art*.

It was left to a new publication, the *Photographic News*, to confront the issues and in their review of the 1859 exhibition to come up with the first hostile criticism.

> In conclusion we may just state, that we are at all times glad to hear of the application of photography to any department of science, but we question the taste of exhibiting all the results. We, therefore, are averse to exhibition of such pictures as the 'Illustrations of Mental Disease'. These photographs ought to adorn the walls of the physician's study, but certainly not the walls of a public exhibition. They are neither interesting as works of art nor as photographs; it is well to know of the application, but we say it again we do not want to see all the results. The photographs are perfectly hideous.[48]

This was the last time that Diamond exhibited his portraits in public. But it would be wrong to see this only as the result of one hostile review. He had resigned his post at the Surrey Asylum in the aftermath of the Dolley Case and had no new photographs to show. Although he had opened his own private asylum in Twickenham, it would have been difficult, with only a dozen patients, to continue a comparative study of insanity which had been based on hundreds of cases. Then, as a friend pointed out, there was the question of propriety, for 'that which was allowable in a public institution would not be so in a private establishment'.[49]

Diamond was not a person to be mentally immobilized by change. His study of insanity had been as much a product of circumstances as was the situation which made him give it up, and he could, after all, leave it with a degree of professional satisfaction. His ambition to see his photographs used to illustrate a medical text-book had been partially fulfilled the previous year when Dr Conolly had used his portraits as the basis of his study of the physiognomy of insanity published in the *Medical Times and Gazette*.[50] It had given him status in medical circles. He had seen other psychiatrists follow his example and introduce photography in their work. As an interest, it was but one of many – one in which he had been successful, and this in turn enhanced his reputation as a photographer. The portraits were proof of his skill. In 1858 he had been elected Secretary of the Photographic Society. In 1859 he became Editor of the *Photographic Journal*. He held both posts until 1869, when he resigned them for health reasons.[51]

But something of the novelty of photography, which had sparked the imagination with a sense of almost limitless possiblities; which had, for a few years, defied categorization either as art or science, rather combining the qualities of both – something of this novelty had worn off. A division had been made. Diamond was known as a technical expert. As a juror of the photographic section of the London International Exhibition in 1862 he published a report in the *Photographic Journal* in which he described photography's changed position:

> For the first time in the crescent of all the arts and sciences, it is recognized as an independent art. In the London Exhibition of 1851, sun pictures were grouped with philosophical instruments; in the Paris Exhibition of 1855, with printing and applied design; so that in the first a photographic landscape was supposed to hang in

its proper place behind a sextant or voltaic battery; in the second among paper-hangings, candlesticks and children's toys. That era of confusion has now been passed, and photography has obtained a distinct place in the arts; it is admitted to rank as a separate class.[52]

It was, as Diamond saw, the end of an era. But the new age which he welcomed, which elected him to many a photographic jury and read, with a degree of interest, his articles on technical developments, was one in which he and his fellow 'pioneers' of applied photography were to be allowed their status as technicians only as a denial of their artistry. From the 1860s until his death in 1886 Dr. Diamond rarely made or exhibited any photographs.

18
The Göschenen entrance to the St. Gotthard Tunnel, 1872 (*Diamond*)

2
The Case of Daniel Dolley

On 9 April 1856, Daniel Dolley, a patient at Springfield, the Surrey County Lunatic Asylum, collapsed shortly after being given a cold shower-bath on the instructions of his physician, Mr Charles Snape, and died only minutes later. A post-mortem examination was held the following day and the report sent to the Coroner by Mr Snape told of extensive heart disease. On 12 April the Coroner's inquest attributed the death to natural causes, and the case would have gone on record simply as that of a sixty-five-year-old patient who died of a heart attack, had not a letter arrived at the offices of the Commissioners in Lunacy, Whitehall, on the day of the inquest.

Surrey Lunatic Asylum
11th April 1856

Gentlemen,
We wish to call your attention to a very dreadful case that took place here on Wednesday, the 9th instant. A patient named Dolley was in an excited state, and Mr Snape was in Nr. 3 ward, and this unfortunate creature struck Mr Snape, but did not hurt him; but Mr Snape ordered Oliver Barnett to give the said person a shower-bath, which he did for twenty-three minutes: three cisterns of water; each cistern contains one ton weight. And after the said person came out of the bath, a large dose of tartar emetic (poison) was forced down his throat; but judge of the effects: the said patient was a corpse in ten minutes after taking the poison; and all this took place without the presence of Mr Snape and by his orders, his horse and chaise waiting at the time to take him to the Crystal Palace. The poison being used at this place requires the immediate attention of yourselves.

We are, etc.
The Attendants of the Surrey County Asylum.
P.S. – An inquest to be held on the body tomorrow, April 12th instant.[1]

19
The main entrance to Springfield Asylum, 1850s

Whoever wrote this letter, for it was not signed by name, apparently believed that Dolley's death, far from being the result of natural causes, involved a degree of negligence and cruelty on the part of Mr Snape which made it necessary to carry out a thorough investigation of his methods. As if predicting the result of the inquest, the authors of the letter had moved beyond the sphere of the Coroner and the local authorities and instantly called in the highest legal power of the lunacy system: the Commissioners in Lunacy.[2]

From one point of view this was the obvious move to make in any such serious case. By 1856 the Commissioners in Lunacy were well known for their inquiries into cases of asylum cruelty. For eleven years they had held the powers to inspect and license all asylums and other institutions housing lunatics such as gaols and workhouses, and to shape the national lunacy system in their reports and recommendations to Parliament. Because of the way they had used these powers – gaining access to asylums where it had previously been denied, rooting out the last remaining cases of systematic malpractice, and lending their support to the campaign for the total abolition of all forms of mechanical restraints in asylums – because of such policies, they had come to be regarded, unofficially, as the legal arm of the reform movement. So taking the case of Dolley as one of pure abuse, it was only to be expected that the authors of this letter should write to the Commissioners in Lunacy.

The letter itself appears extraordinary only after taking into account the circumstances under which it was written. Considering the date and the place from which it came, its tone is curiously out of date – perhaps by as little as five years, yet still noticeably so. It is a letter full of the secrecy of the old asylum scandals, with elements of fear and violence woven through, telling of poison being forced down the patient's throat. There is something almost furtive in its anonymity – which can find no other access to justice than by such hysterical whisperings.

Yet this is a letter written in 1856, when as far as psychiatry was concerned, the violence of the previous centuries had been halted – when the long wished-for reforms in the treatment of mental patients had in fact been implemented, and on such a heroic scale that many reformers, naturally enough, considered themselves safely divorced from the more brutal practices of the past. Lord Shaftesbury had written, as early as 1847:

> It is remarkable and very humiliating, the long and tedious process by which we have arrived at the sound practice of the treatment of the insane, which now appears to be the suggestion of common sense and ordinary humanity.[3]

Yet reading this letter in his official capacity as Chairman of the Lunacy Commission, Shaftesbury could have been forgiven a momentary doubt as to whether or not the reforms for which he and his fellows had fought for thirty years and seen accomplished so recently had ever in fact been carried out. For this letter came, not from some distant, unconverted outpost of the lunacy system, but from the centre of the reformed sector: from a large county asylum on the edge of London.

Yet, if the very tone of this letter seemed to query some of the reformers' purest assumptions, the outcome of the whole case would prove to be far more disruptive. Some of the questions it raised, on issues of psychiatric treatment, and the power structure of the new asylum system, were to be answered in a way which implicitly challenged some of psychiatry's most important achievements of the previous decades.

What had been achieved in the first half of the century? The case of Dolley occurred in the Surrey County Lunatic Asylum – and county asylums were one of the measures of progress in nineteenth-century psychiatry.

The bill passed by Parliament in 1845 laying down the powers of the Lunacy Commission had as its twin one which required all counties to set up public asylums for their pauper lunatics. It was an act which gave the official stamp of law to the reformers' campaign to assign responsibility for the care and protection of the insane to society as a whole and to give such responsibility the specific form – not of certifying patients and detaining them in gaols or workhouses, as had so often previously happened – but of providing a coherent system of shelter, sustenance and medical treatment. Though by the time this bill was passed several counties had already made some such provision, the law, as well as requiring the remainder to follow suit, officially declared the right of pauper lunatics to this form of public support and, taking up a humanitarian stance, sanctioned the development of psychiatry as a valid branch of medicine. At the same time, the law provided in the Lunacy Commission an administrative machine to oversee the running of such a system.

The asylums were to provide treatment for their inmates – and the question of treatment was inevitably bound up with that of *non-restraint*. Many of the county asylums, including Springfield, had opened when the belief was still widely held that mechnical restraints were indispensable as asylum equipment. Psychiatrists in several of the old institutions, holding hard to the traditional methods of straitjackets, straps and iron-cuffs to subdue their patients, offered a precedent which was all too often taken up and refined as a supposed form of treatment in the new asylums.

The rights of a predominantly lay body like the Lunacy Commission to interfere in questions of professional practice were distinctly limited. True, half a century earlier, the movement in England to abolish restraints had first sprung out of a purely philanthropic initiative on the part of a group of Quakers in York who under the leadership of a merchant, William Tuke, had set up their own asylum, The Retreat,[4] in opposition to the penal methods of physicians and keepers in the old York Asylum.[5] Philanthropists could always oppose cases of pure abuse – so it proved comparatively straightforward for the commissioners to challenge and eliminate the use of restraints when there was no reason other than laziness or vindictiveness for their application – cases reminiscent of the notorious history of Norris, who had been discovered in 1814 in the basement of the old Bethlem Asylum where he had been kept bolted to the wall in a curious iron construction for at least ten years by a drunken keeper.[6] It was far simpler for the commissioners, once they had gained access to all asylums, to abolish such instances than to contradict the professional opinion of those psychiatrists who favoured restraints as a form of treatment.

The fact that by the 1850s restraints had been abolished from Britain's public asylums was due largely to the practice of a few enlightened physicians who, grasping the humanitarian spirit of Tuke's example, extended it into a scientific principle. Among them was Dr John Conolly, who within four months of taking up the post of Resident Physician at the Middlesex

20
William Norris in his cell at Bethlem Hospital, May 1814

Asylum, Hanwell in 1839 (at that time the largest in the country with more than 800 patients) had abolished all restraints throughout the asylum. He had come to recognize not only the inhumanity of subduing patients by force but also the futility of such methods in terms of effecting a cure. To use restraints, Conolly argued, only showed 'the coarse determination of vain and ignorant men to effect by force what they could not accomplish by science' – for whatever the method of restraint, its effect always was only to restrain the patients' movements – quite disregarding 'the source of irritation in the brain'. The use of force and violence, he argued, was not only an affront to humanity, it also aggravated the patients' mental states. To abolish all coercive methods, to replace force with the principle of

24

21
Springfield Asylum, 1841

kindness, was not just the natural right of patients, it also created a situation in which the symptoms of a patient's disorder could be seen unaggravated, and so opened up psychiatry to scientific study while offering patients real and restoring refuge in an asylum.[7]

These were some of the principles which had come to dominate psychiatric theory and practice by the 1850s, and according to which all public asylums were said to be run. They amounted in essence to what Shaftesbury had called 'ordinary humanity and common sense'. How such principles were put into practice in asylums – something of how non-restraint psychiatry actually worked – is examined in the next part of this book. It is sufficient at this point to say that, in 1852, when the commissioners polled the opinion of all psychiatrists in public

asylums, the response was unanimously in favour of non-restraint. Perhaps for public employees it would have been unwise to disagree with such a widely approved policy, but certainly Diamond was not the only convert to the new system, and in reply to the commissioners he wrote:

> In a properly constructed building, with a sufficient number of suitable attendants, restraint is never necessary, never justifiable, and always injurious, in all cases of lunacy whatever; and this is quite the reverse of my former ideas, when my knowledge of the treatment of insanity was much more limited than at the present time.[8]

Non-restraint was approved and accepted but, as Diamond saw, such a practice was intrinsically bound up with the asylum itself, its facilities and the way in which it was run. The

25

new methods under which hundreds of patients were to be supervised without any recourse to mechanical coercion depended on adequate resources in terms of staff, space, accommodation etc. So what were the resources of the county asylums, and how were they run?

The Surrey Magistrates had opened their asylum, Springfield, in 1841 when only fifteen of the fifty-five counties of England and Wales had made any such provision for their pauper lunatics. It opened after five years of planning and preparation as something of a showpiece.[9] The asylum building was 'in the Tudor style of architecture' set in an estate of almost 100 acres on the edge of Wandsworth Common with a farm and several workshops, for manual labour was already used as treatment in cases of insanity and, as the managing committee pointed out, the money earned or saved this way 'helped to diminish the pecuniary charges of the establishment'.[10] This Committee of Visiting Justices had been appointed by the Surrey Magistrates – first to plan the asylum and subsequently to manage its affairs. Running the asylum was a part-time, unpaid, voluntary occupation for the committee members – yet they wielded immense authority, for the committee not only controlled the asylum's finances, it also laid down the asylum's regulations, appointed and dismissed all staff, visited the wards, inspected the case-books and officially sanctioned the admission and discharge of patients. Each member of the staff, from the ward attendants to the maintenance staff, through to the physicians themselves, was answerable to the committee. The committee was answerable to the Surrey Magistrates who, as representatives of the rate-payers, allocated the asylum's finances from the county rates.

In planning such a philanthropic venture it would be unfair to accuse the committee of any meanness. They planned what they believed to be a model asylum for 350 patients – little thinking that once it was opened so many more pauper lunatics, whose very existence had been unknown, would suddenly appear as if from nowhere to sample the benefits of asylum life.[11] And if subsequently the committee's concern with economy in running the asylum seems to have overridden their initial philanthropic

ideas – was it not as representatives of the rate-payers who, while priding themselves on making such provisions for their paupers, could still resent as altogether unnecessary the demand that such provision made on their purses?[12]

Certainly, for some such reason, by the 1850s when Dr Diamond and Mr Snape held the posts of Resident Physicians at the Surrey Asylum, a tradition of overcrowding and understaffing had long since set in.[13] There were usually as many as 800 patients in residence, though comparatively little planned expansion had taken place in the asylum's accommodation. Before any extensions were made to the buildings, basements and other rooms designed as workshops or places for exercise in wet weather had been converted into dormitories and filled with patients. Under such conditions Diamond and Snape were asked to manage their patients according to the system of non-restraint.

What made this situation still more difficult for the physicians was that though under this system a well-ordered asylum formed a crucial part of the patients' treatment, the physicians' influence over the way it was run was limited. The committee allocated them duties while denying them power to make important decisions. Dr Diamond in the female department and Mr Snape in the male were each often in charge of as many as 400 patients – yet the first duty laid down for them by the committee was to visit and inspect their wards twice a day and every patient at least once a day. Their other duties ranged from the charge of all drugs and medicine to the duty to encourage attendance at chapel. They were to keep the registers and case-books, prescribe any special diets, decide which patients should work, provide exercise for those who could not be employed and generally direct 'the care, instruction, and the amusement of all'.

Given this concept of the physician's role, perhaps it was not to be expected that he should have any say in the larger administrative questions of finance and expenditure, or in planning what facilities the asylum would offer. Yet on a more particularly professional level, physicians like Diamond and Snape had no say in the admission of patients and could not discharge them without the committee's approval. Though they were to supervise the ward attendants, on whom their work depended to an extraordinary degree, they had no say in deciding who was to be employed for this work and who dismissed. And, in the case of an asylum like Springfield where the male and female departments were run independently by their two physicians, the degree of dependence on its authority which the committee exerted militated against any professional co-operation between the physicians. Each department was a law unto itself. Diamond and Snape, in so far as they were given any authority at all, used it each in his own province as he saw best, under the constant surveillance of the Committee of Visitors.

So, turning to the case of Daniel Dolley and taking into account the immense authority of the Committee of Visitors and the responsibility this gave them for all matters concerning the Surrey Asylum, we see that, natural though it was for the authors of this anonymous letter to address themselves to the commissioners, for the commissioners not to report the letter back to the Committee of Visitors amounted among other things to a breach in protocol.

But the commissioners were not looking at the case from that point of view. Called upon to investigate a case of abuse, they responded to the secrecy of their informants. They applied to the Coroner for a transcript of the evidence heard at the inquest and to Mr Snape for a copy of his account of the post-mortem examination and set up a private inquiry into the death of Daniel Dolley.

Mr Snape was not called to give his account of the case. The witnesses examined by the commissioners, with Lord Shaftesbury chairing the proceedings, were the ward attendants who had been involved in the case – and Dr Diamond.

As far as the material facts were concerned, the story told by the attendants corroborated that of the anonymous letter, but it was presented without any assumptions of cruelty or any accusations against Mr Snape. No one referred to tartar emetic as 'poison'. The suggestion that force had been used in giving either the shower-bath or the emetic was denied.

According to one attendant, John Oliver Barnett, Dolley had been unusually excited on the morning of the incident, and unusually abusive to the other patients, one of whom he had struck: 'I think it very rarely occurred to me to see him so jocular; he was so light-hearted: dancing, and such things.' So when Mr Snape arrived to inspect the ward he was instantly informed of Dolley's state:

Mr Snape of course called him by his name, and he became very abusive and threatening. Mr Snape said, 'Come this way, Dolley,' and he went towards the shower-bath, and he then up with his fist, and struck Mr Snape on the side of the head, and gave him a very violent blow, and then went to run through No.2 ward.[14]

Barnett and two other attendants had stopped Dolley, taken him to the shower-bath and undressed him. Dolley had then walked into the bath himself quite calmly.

After I had him in, and the bar down, Mr Snape says, 'Now, pull the string, Barnett,' that is the string for the water to come down, and then Mr Snape said to me, he said, 'Barnett, I never was struck by a patient before since I have been in the institution,' he stayed for a moment or two, and said, 'Keep him in half an hour.'

According to Barnett, Mr Snape had then left with the instruction to 'look in upon him several times'. When the half hour was almost up, he had let Dolley out, rubbed him down, helped him to dress and then taken him to the day-room where, sitting in a fireside chair, he had been given as Mr Snape had instructed 'a good dose of the light-coloured mixture' (tartar emetic). One attendant had helped Dolley to put on his socks, another went to fetch him some slippers, and it was then, less than than ten minutes after leaving the shower-bath, that Dolley appeared to have gone into a sort of fit. He was carried to a bed, Mr Snape was summoned and came immediately, but he found Dolley dead. This then was the story told by the attendants.

The commissioners asked if extended shower-baths were ever given as punishment; they asked if Mr Snape had shown anger when ordering this one – whether, in other words, it had been ordered as punishment for the blow Dolley had struck him. All such suggestions were denied. True, the attendants considered half an hour an unusually long time for a shower-bath, but they had noticed no unusual reaction on the part of the patient at the time – Dolley had shivered, but even after short baths, all the patients did that.

The commissioners moved on to question Dr Diamond. He had first heard of the case, how Dolley had struck Mr Snape, been given a half-hour bath and died directly afterwards – he had heard all this from Mr Snape himself.

> I thought from what he said that there was some disease of the heart, and I told him I hoped the shower-bath had not been the cause of the death; and, in fact, I did not think very seriously of it at that time. I then said to him, 'Whenever you make the post-mortem examination I will assist you.' I then went round the male wards in the evening, and I asked Barnett to see Dolley's body. I was very much astonished to see it, for it was as white as the marble; it was like a piece of alabaster.
>
> COMMISSIONERS: The whole of the circulation had moved from the surface?
>
> DIAMOND: Entirely so, and I asked Barnett, in a way not to excite his suspicion, for I thought it an unpleasant occurrence, if he would tell me the particulars, and he told me that which I was not aware of before, that as soon as he came from the bath he had given him a good dose, as an emetic, and he died directly afterwards.

As a result of this discovery Diamond had written to Snape that he now found the case to be more serious than he had supposed and he advised him to discuss it with the Committee of Visitors as soon as possible. The following day Diamond had attended the post-mortem, taking with him his eldest son, Warren Hasting Diamond, who as a recent graduate of the College of Surgeons was asked by Snape to perform the operation. The two physicians then examined Dolley's heart.

What had they found? 'We argued it at the time of the post-mortem examination,' said Diamond. 'Mr Snape thought that there was more disease than I did myself.' Diamond for his part had been unable to detect any disease in the heart itself and thought that the deterioration of some of the valves was only such as would be found in anyone of that age. 'I do not think there was any disease of the heart to cause death,' he said, 'but I am sorry to say I think the bath did cause death in conjunction with the tartar emetic afterwards.' After checking through Mr Snape's account of the post-mortem

examination and hearing in greater detail the grounds for Dr Diamond's disagreement, the commissioners returned to his conclusion, asking:

> Then your opinion is, that the cause of death was the bath, followed by the tartar emetic?
>
> DIAMOND: I have no doubt of it. I had a conversation with Mr Snape previous to the inquest, and I told him he must manage so that I should not be examined, because I felt so strongly upon the subject.
>
> COMMISSIONERS: You advised him not to call you as a witness?
>
> DIAMOND: I advised him not to call me. I took a walk at the time of the inquest.
>
> COMMISSIONERS: Did you state the reason why you advised him not to call you as a witness?
>
> DIAMOND: A few words did occur, but really I cannot say exactly what they were. The truth was, we did not think alike.

Their inquiry convinced the commissioners of the necessity of taking further action. On 19 April they sent a transcript of the evidence they had heard to the Committee of Visitors, warning that the facts involved 'a charge of very grave character against Mr Snape', and they invited the committee somewhat belatedly to submit their comments.

The committee was not inclined to co-operate. An investigation into the death of a patient at the Surrey Asylum had taken place without its knowledge and in the absence of Mr Snape – a proceeding it considered 'completely at variance with every principle of justice and propriety'.[15] The committee declined to make any move until the question of criminal proceeding was decided. The commissioners replied that manslaughter was the charge involved. The committee then suspended Mr Snape from office.

Faced with criminal proceedings, Mr Snape applied to the commissioners for permission to exhume Dolley's body. He would re-examine the heart. The commissioners replied by sending a copy of the following letter:

> Surrey County Lunatic Asylum,
> near Wansworth
> 17 May 1856
>
> Gentlemen,
> In compliance with Mr Law's wish, I beg to inform you that the circumstances connected with the removal of Dolley's heart are as follows:
> On Monday morning the 14th of April, my son, by my direction, brought me the heart, which I was

anxious, for my own satisfaction, and with a view to form a correct judgement, to examine with more minuteness than I had previously had an opportunity of doing. I did examine it on that day, and kept it until the Thursday, on which day I met the Reverend J.B. Reade, Vicar of Stone, near Aylesbury, and Chaplain to the Bucks Asylum, in company with Mr Waterhouse, one of the Visiting Justices of the York Asylum, to whom I communicated what I had done. Mr Reade advised me to show it to Mr Paget, which I did: I also showed it to Mr Hancock.

In consequence of a suggestion of Mr Paget, I on the following day submitted portions of it to the microscope, which portions I have retained. The heart itself having become very offensive, I on Saturday evening, the 19th instant, covered it with ashes and burnt it in my surgery fire.

It did not at the time occur to me that I was violating any rule, and I regret extremely if I have done so.

I am etc.
(*signed*) Hugh W. Diamond[16]

On 16 June, Mr Charles Snape appeared at Bow Street Magistrate's Court charged 'for that he did feloniously kill and slay one Daniel Dolley'. After hearing the evidence presented to support this charge – from the ward attendants and Dr Diamond – evidence concerning the shower-bath at the Surrey Asylum, and the opinions of various psychiatrists who disapproved of Snape's methods, the Magistrate committed the defendant for trial at the Old Bailey.[17]

The Commissioners in Lunacy, as the legal representatives of the 'poor lunatic', had been called to investigate a case of abuse. They had summoned witnesses and taken their evidence – yet in many ways this evidence was more ambiguous than they had cared to admit. It presented the case in terms of treatment – treatment which in a milder form was widely used at Springfield, and which must therefore have already come to the attention of the commissioners in their asylum inspections; treatment which in an extreme form, Diamond believed, had caused Dolley's death – but nevertheless a form of treatment.

Yet this evidence, rather than prompting them to examine the medical basis of Snape's methods, seems only to have confirmed the commissioners in their initial attitude when setting up their inquiry. The law rather than medicine was their province. Instead of opening up the case to a public inquiry or summoning

Mr Snape to explain his methods, they had called up the full weight of the law and directed it – not so much at the treatment given to Dolley as at Mr Snape himself. With the charge of manslaughter they set themselves to prove not only that extended shower-baths used in conjunction with emetics endangered life, but also what Mr Snape's motives had been in prescribing them. The death of Daniel Dolley was, in other words, to be presented and argued as an old-style case of abuse. Perhaps the past, from which in theory the new lunacy system had divorced itself, was still too recent, too immediate to be forgotten, and the efforts of the reformers to allocate responsibility to various authorities had somehow created a situation of mutual distrust.

What then did all this mean for Dr Diamond, who was now about to be called as a key witness for the prosecution? 'The truth was we did not think alike' – of any more concrete truths Diamond had said nothing. He had given his opinion to the commissioners emphatically, but as opinion only. The condition of Dolley's heart had been open to debate – he and Snape had argued it at the post-mortem but without coming to any agreement. Since Mr Snape's position as physician to the male department authorized him to report his version to the Coroner – what could Diamond do? If he felt that there was more to tell he had certainly shown no interest in telling the Coroner or in arguing the case with Snape in public at the inquest. Diamond's first interest was to find out for himself the cause of Dolley's death – so with a complete disregard for the legalities and formalities of such a case, he had sent his son to collect Dolley's heart. As in so many of his other scientific projects, the truth, for Diamond, was something to be arrived at independently through his own researches or in consultation with experts. Apparently forgetful of his accountability to any higher authority, he had of his own initiative taken the heart to the surgeons Paget and Hancock. He had told them nothing of the circumstances of Dolley's death, and their opinion of the heart, reluctant though they were to comment without more precise information about various related circumstances, had corresponded with his.

It is impossible to say what Diamond would have done had the commissioners not then been summoned to the case. But certainly the commissioners' actions in carrying out a private inquiry and instituting criminal proceedings against Mr Snape took up Diamond's initiative and channelled it into the prosecution camp. The opinions of Diamond, Paget and Hancock were to be used to prove Mr Snape's guilt on a charge of manslaughter - and with such a charge there would be little room for impartial medical debate.

As the prosecution and defence prepared their cases for the confrontation, everyone involved must have been aware of the weighty implications of any evidence they gave. This could be why the ward attendant who had given the dose of emetic now remembered that Dolley had spat half of it into the fire - and Dr Diamond was unable to recall the substance of the conversation he had had with Mr Snape about his not appearing at the Coroner's inquest.

The press had picked up the case at the Magistrate's Court and presented it as a return to the bad old days of restraint, convicting Mr Snape of cruelty before his trial had begun.[18] The medical profession, seeing dangerous consequences in such reports, continued the public debate. The *Journal of Mental Science* published an article on the legal implications of such an approach. The Editor commented:

> If a medical man can be put on his trial for manslaughter, because the life of a patient is lost on account of any treatment honestly prescribed by him, the hands of medical science will be effectually tied, and any step beyond the limits of the narrowest routine will be condemned and avoided by the profession as leading its members into danger and disgrace.[19]

The article commented that the prosecution would have to establish what Mr Snape's motives were when he prescribed the treatment. Quoting Mr Snape's remark - 'I have never been struck by a patient before. Keep him in half an hour, and give him a dose of the light-coloured mixture' - the article concluded:

> Upon this expression the counsel for the prosecution endeavours to take the treatment out of the category of erroneous judgement, and to place it in that of criminal motive, namely, the motive to revenge a blow by a dangerous punishment which proved fatal. Without

this expression there could have been no case.

Meanwhile prosecution and defence canvassed the opinion of medical experts and collected statements to support their cases. Those physicians who were prepared to testify for the prosecution all recorded surprise that treatment of this kind had been employed. Standard practice, they said, was to use the shower-bath as a stimulant, to rouse 'the dormant and flagging powers of the mind' and to give 'tone' to the nervous system. Such a bath would last on average between two and three minutes and consist of not more than fifteen to eighteen gallons of water. 'The benefit,' said one, 'consists in the shock.' Opinion was unanimous among these physicians, who included some of the most prominent practitioners of non-restraint psychiatry, that such an extended bath as that which had been given to Dolley would have a lowering rather than a stimulating effect and would, almost certainly, result in death:

> . . . Witness has borne in mind the fact that Dolley was a lunatic; that insane persons will suffer what sane persons cannot; that they will go through frost and snow, and not be hurt; and what would kill a sane person, an insane person would go through without being hurt; that the fact of Dolley's being insane, does not, however, alter the opinion of witness as to the cause of his death . . . [statement of John Elliotson MD, extract from prosecution brief].[20]

When the case finally came up at the Old Bailey at the beginning of July, even the Judge seems to have shared in the general confusion as to how it should be dealt with. Presenting the case to the grand jury he was hesitant about the charge of manslaughter and offered his assessment of the treatment - he considered shower-baths far preferable to the old methods of chains and other restraints for 'lowering patients' and thought it would be necessary to inquire 'if the treatment adopted by Mr Snape was accompanied by a reasonable degree of knowledge of his profession, attention and caution. 'God forbid,' said the Judge, 'that any medical man should be rendered liable to charge of manslaughter for a mere mistake.'[21] For various technical reasons the case was then adjourned, but when the court reconvened in mid-September the Judge appeared to believe the case more complex and serious than he had supposed and urged the grand jury 'to find the bill', so that the whole case could be thoroughly investigated by the petty jury.[22]

How much of the case, one wonders, was to be based on fact and how much on opinion?

What were the facts?

On 9 April 1856, Daniel Dolley, a patient at the Surrey County Lunatic Asylum, had collapsed shortly after being given a cold shower-bath on the instructions of his physician, Mr Charles Snape, and died only minutes later.

> The bath is a wooden box, 19 inches square, 8 feet 3 inches high, having a solid wooden door, without aperture of any kind. The patient having entered this box, the door is fastened by a strong iron bar on the outside. The perforated plate admitting the shower is pierced with holes, about one-sixth of an inch in diameter, at intervals of six-eighths of an inch, and so arranged that the water descending at a rate varying from 19½–39 gallons per minute, completely envelops the patient, fills the centre of the box, and thus expels the atmospheric air [Henry Hancock, surgeon, Charing Cross Hospital].[23]

Civil engineers, Charles Vignolles and W. Shields, had calculated that during the twenty-eight minute shower-bath, 618 gallons of cold water fell on Daniel Dolley. James Glaisher of the Meteorological Department, Greenwich, had reported that the temperature on 9 April had been 45° Fahrenheit:

> ... the effect of water, at the temperature of 45°, falling upon and over the human body, would be to reduce that body rapidly, as every drop of water which came in contact with it would take some heat away. This action, together with that by rapid evaporation, causing a further loss of heat, would be followed by a very marked and painful sensation of cold.[24]

The grand jury, presented with a bill of indictment against Mr Snape, examined some of the witnesses for the prosecution – and promptly threw out the bill as 'not found'. The law had decided that the death of Daniel Dolley did not involve any criminal action on the part of Mr Snape, and the legal case was closed.

Where did this leave the question of extended shower-bath treatments? Little of the medical evidence had been heard, and none of Mr Snape's defence. The question of treatment, hardly touched on in the proceedings, had slipped through the legal framework and

remained unresolved – though by implication sharing in Mr Snape's acquittal. With the case thrown out of court, the Commissioners in Lunacy had no real alternative but to withdraw from the debate. They had staked their authority on the manslaughter charge, and the acquittal cost them dear in terms of credibility. In their final statement, though obviously dissatisfied with the outcome, they consoled themselves with the observation that the publicity of such a trial would act as a deterrent to the introduction of any similar practices in other asylums. They said nothing about the negative implications of the case – nor anything about the situation which now existed at the Surrey Asylum. Internal asylum politics lay outside their jurisdiction.

Power to decide the future of Mr Snape now came back to the Committee of Visiting Justices, but it came rather late in the affair and with an inevitable backlog of hostility. The committee too would hold its own inquiry. It asked Mr Snape to submit his account of the case which it would consider, together with some of the prosecution evidence, under the guidance of six eminent physicians – three to be selected by the committee and three by Mr Snape. Naturally enough none of the physicians who had previously chosen to testify for the commissioners was selected. The trial had polarized opinion irrevocably – and upon the acquittal, as the pivot of the whole affair, power to attack had swung back to the defendant. At last Mr Snape was given the opportunity to answer the commissioners' accusations. He wrote to the committee:

> I rejoice at being enabled to lay before you the real facts relative to Dolley's treatment and death, being confident that you will enter upon the investigation fully prepared to do no less justice to myself and family, than to those unfortunate beings whose interests are entrusted to your care.[25]

Safely acquitted by the grand jury, Mr Snape none the less found himself financially ruined by loss of salary and the costs of his defence. In his statement to the committee, which ran to many thousands of words, he reacted as a man who had long been cornered professionally and socially, throwing his punches in all directions. Not content simply to offer an explanation of his methods, he set about justifying every circumstance connected with Dolley's death – unable to voice the slightest regret that his patient had died. He presented the case of Dolley as an example of his personal discovery – his new system of extended shower-baths for purposes of sedation. At the same time he had much to say about Dr Diamond:

> Whilst laying before you the case of Dolley, I have deemed it incumbent on me to notice certain allegations in Dr Diamond's evidence, taken in my absence before the Commissioners of Lunacy, which question the judiciousness of my mode of treatment, as well as tend to show a difference of practice in the two departments, much to my prejudice. I am compelled, therefore, to refer in my statement to the practice pursued by Dr Diamond in the establishment . . .

Not only had he, Snape, used extended shower-baths and strong emetics on previous occasions with good effect – so too, he insisted, had Diamond, though testifying to the contrary. And Diamond's doses of emetic were stronger than his – and so Snape continued through many a detail of Diamond's evidence.

In the case of Dolley, Snape denied that he had been 'influenced by vindictive motives against the deceased' when specifying the duration of the bath. The remark, 'I never was struck by a patient before', far from being a reason for ordering punishment,

> . . . was uttered only as an exclamation, implying that the patient must have been most unusually excited to act so insubordinately, inasmuch as the patients, being all paupers, are usually most respectful; and I, therefore, after deliberating, considered it necessary to meet such unusual excitement, in a man whom I knew to be *dangerous when excited*, by stronger treatment than I had previously applied.

Dolley's death, Snape claimed, had been caused by 'fatty degeneration of the heart' and exhaustion following extreme cerebral excitement. Dr Diamond himself had advised him after the post-mortem to tell the Coroner that the man had 'just such a heart where you would expect sudden death to arise'. Diamond's subsequent investigation of the heart, Snape felt, was too obviously unethical to require further comment.

Confident that the treatment given to Dolley was 'justifiable in itself', Snape now announced that he had been developing this method of sedation over many years without any ill effects:

> The fact is, that there is a principle of resistance in the physical and nervous condition of the lunatic which would often require three times the counter application requisite for the same patient if sane.

In reply to those critics who saw such methods as an infringement of the principles of non-restraint, Snape declared his support for the non-restraint system – 'in the largest sense of that phrase'. But, with a definition of this system which emphasized its care of patients but ignored the remedial possibilities of such caring, Snape stated his belief in a higher duty than that of following non-restraint – that of curing patients – and he defended his shower-bath treatments as an important discovery for medical science:

> If on the 8th April I had announced to the public my practice of the previous five years, I should have probably received from my colleagues – not condemnation, but high approval: and 'continuous baths' would then have been recognized as one of the 'fresh sources' so desired to be possessed by the practitioner for the cure of the disease of the brain.

This then was the substance of Mr Snape's defence.

The medical authorities chosen by Mr Snape and the committee were unanimous in the opinion that Mr Snape had been justified in his treatment of Daniel Dolley.[26] As Mr Snape had pointed out – had they found otherwise, would any Medical Superintendent ever venture to try out new treatments?

The final word on the case came from the Committee of Visitors, almost a year after Dolley's death, in a report to the Home Secretary.[27] This report, apart from Mr Snape's defence statement, which it included, was almost entirely taken up with criticisms of the way in which the various inquiries had been conducted. It was the committee's turn to answer the Commissioners in Lunacy. The committee objected to the secrecy of the initial inquiry and the manner of questioning witnesses, not only as being unjust to Mr Snape, but as an unwarranted, irregular intrusion into asylum affairs. The fact that the commissioners had not first consulted the committee implied a criticism of their management. The committee had thus shared in the insult of secrecy and the disgrace of criminal proceedings.

With reference to the conduct of the two medical officers, the committee first reported its opinion of Mr Snape – that, 'in several particulars, as represented in the evidence, the conduct of Mr Snape in this unfortunate case was not unobjectionable', but that after considering his defence, the committee had decided to reinstate Snape in his post as Resident Physician.

Real dissatisfaction was reserved for Dr Diamond – not least, one suspects, because Diamond had made no effort to appease the committee. The committee had wanted to know why he had not appeared at the Coroner's inquest? Why he had carried out a private investigation and then destroyed Dolley's heart? Why he had given his opinion of the case to the commissioners, not the committee? Diamond apparently had nothing more to say. So it was on the conduct of Dr Diamond that the committee pronounced the following verdict:

The Committee cannot too deeply lament that a

proceeding, so devoid of those honourable and delicate feelings they confidently trusted might have been relied on in a medical officer of their own, should have occurred in the Asylum. After a full inquiry and consideration of Dr Diamond's defence, the Committee came to the conclusion 'that in many instances he had made himself liable to severe reprehension', and they requested their chairman 'to express to him the animadversion of the committee', which was done accordingly.

The case was finally closed. The staff at the Surrey Asylum had returned to their duties. Mr Snape was once more responsible for the male patients, Dr Diamond for the females – both directly answerable to the Committee of Visiting Justices.

What then had come from the case of Daniel Dolley?

The Committee of Visiting Justices informed its medical officers that in future the precise duration of all shower-baths was to be entered in the case-books. This was the only positive result of the entire business.

Mr Snape had been reinstated as Resident Physican. His challenge to the principles of non-restraint had finally escaped criticism, primarily

22
Twickenham House, from an advertisement, 1870

because he had presented it under the auspices of medical treatment. Rather than simply *caring* for patients, had he not said that he preferred to *cure* them? Of course he had addressed such observations to his Committee of Visitors, whose own authority had been temporarily shaken by the events of the trial; he addressed them as a group of laymen – and argued his own authority as a physician. What his medical opponents would have made of his claims is another matter. Their opinions were never publicly heard. The question of Mr Snape's shower-bath treatments was never fully, impartially debated.

And what of the Committee of Visiting Justices?

The case of Daniel Dolley had indeed taken place in one of those large public asylums on the edge of London, at the very heart of the reformed sector of the asylum system. But the process of reform had brought with it a new set of problems. The system of non-restraint depended on the resources of the asylum – but how were these asylums, increasingly over-crowded, often with more than 1,000 patients –

how were they to be run? In such large-scale institutions how was authority for the various medical and administrative matters to be allocated, given that all such issues were so interrelated? As early as 1844, Conolly had found himself forced to resign his post as Resident Physician at Hanwell (though he continued as Visiting Physician) precisely because of conflict with his committee on such questions.[28] Was the unity of the reform movement to be undermined by political manoeuvrings and administrative muddles?

After the case of Daniel Dolley, the Committee of Visiting Justices to the Surrey Asylum found itself confirmed in its role of guardian to pauper lunatics, secure in the conviction that it alone had not overstepped the bounds of its authority. But did no one question whether the range and extent of that authority was fully justified?

Early in 1858 Dr Diamond handed his resignation to the Committee of Visitors and, leaving Springfield, he moved to Twickenham where he opened his own private asylum.

3
The Physiognomy of Insanity

Dr Diamond's portraits of his patients are very much the product of non-restraint psychiatry – of those principles of 'ordinary humanity and common sense' from which the case of Daniel Dolley represented such a falling off. He made them when these principles had already won the abolition of all mechnical restraints and made it

23
Dr Conolly, 1857 (*Diamond*)

possible for an asylum to become literally a refuge for its inmates. He made them in the years before the bureaucratic ideals of order and efficiency had come to approve the introduction of the equally coercive use of drugs working directly on a patient's nervous system (a practice later referred to by Conolly's son-in-law, Sir Henry Maudsley, as 'chemical restraint').[1] They belong to the centre of a period of scarcely thirty years during which the control of mental patients could not, so simply, be enforced by their physicians.

County asylums such as Springfield had brought together unprecedented numbers of people classed as insane. Some were society's unacceptables: the blind, deaf, dumb or mentally retarded; a large proportion were old, incurable patients who would remain there for life and whose care took up the greater part of an asylum's resources. They were all paupers. For psychiatrists, the problems of overcrowding and understaffing often meant that much of their time was taken up with a mass of administrative duties. Yet despite strenuous, often frustrating, working conditions, many of them retained sufficient optimism to try out new therapies and methods of treatment in order to further scientific knowledge of insanity. The asylum era itself was still young and experimental, and when experiment formed a part of true non-restraint practice, the somewhat eclectic methods adopted by psychiatrists not only brought tangible improvements in their patients' conditions, but also saw remarkable results in terms of *cures*.

To abolish restraints had meant to rethink

24

The Royal Hospital of Bethlem: The Gallery for Women, 1860

methods of treatment completely. The non-restraint movement had focused attention on the way the use of force not only aggravated mental suffering, but also precluded any scientific study of insanity, and once the instruments of restraint and the treatments associated with them were removed from asylums, very little remained in the way of medical precedent upon which psychiatrists could base their patients' treatment.[2] The ideal for the future was to build up the body of clinical knowledge with which to develop psychiatry scientifically. The problem for the present was to run asylums and care for the patients who were already there.[3] Confronted with this immediate problem, but also with daily examples of how much their patients had benefited from the abolition of restraints, psychiatrists began to consider whether, even when they were unable to diagnose disease with any degree of confidence, the mental disturbances of their patients might be alleviated by further improvements in their physical and material conditions.[4]

The majority of patients in any public asylum had exhausted their energies in the effort to keep alive in or out of the workhouse. Whatever the immediate causes of insanity, in this respect their histories were singularly alike. As a result, psychiatrists came to regard the debilitating effects of poverty as a crucial factor in the majority of cases and saw a potential remedy in asylum life itself. Conolly said:

> To be well clothed, to have a comfortable bed and sufficient good food every day may, of course, be considered as having peculiarly comforting effects on pauper patients, too long accustomed to scanty fare, and miserable lodging, and wretched clothing. They often come to the asylum half starved, and good food is not infrequently of far more consequence to them than medicine of any kind.

Reading such comments gives a new perspective on the many recorded cases of patients who were unwilling to leave asylums. To suggest that they had simply succumbed to institutionalization ignores the working and living conditions into which they were being discharged.

25
The Royal Hospital of Bethlem: The Gallery for Men. 1860

Whatever the other failings of psychiatry at that time, when society at large had hardly begun to consider the welfare of the poor, public asylums offered their inmates a standard of living which was so often an improvement on that from which they came.

But asylums were not simply places of refuge. Treatment and management, then as now, were inseparable and non-restraint emphasized restoring patients to health as opposed to keeping them in safe custody and suppressing their symptoms. Under a true non-restraint system humane principles and the pursuit of scientific knowledge supported each other to the benefit both of the patients and of science. It was to be all too easy, as subsequent developments in asylum history show, for *carers* to become *keepers* again when the stimulus of psychiatric research was withdrawn from these institutions. But in the 1850s the asylum was still an organic unit with potential for new life and growth.

It offered a unique opportunity for the comparative study of insanity on a large scale at a time when psychiatry was still ignored in general medical education and there were no psychiatric units in general hospitals. Not only could thousands of patients be observed, but some of the legalization designed for their protection regulating, for example, the keeping of admission and discharge records and case-books, had begun to produce an unprecedented quantity of data on mental illness. Asylum physicians were at the very source of psychiatric activities and advances in the mid-nineteenth century. In 1841 they had founded the Association of Medical Officers of Asylums and Hospitals for the Insane (now the Royal College of Psychiatrists) and their publications, the *Asylum Journal of Medical Science* and the *Journal of Psychological Medicine* were focusing points for psychiatric debate.

Non-restraint psychiatry can best be understood by looking at its practice – at the way in which the attitude of these physicians found expression in the details of institutional life. Take, for example, their system of classification:

26a

Acute Mania (*Esquirol, 1838*)

26b

The same patient, convalescent (*Esquirol, 1838*)

rather than attempting, on insufficient evidence, to name diseases, classification was based on the symptoms displayed by the patients – a system which contributed both to the scientific search for order and to the orderliness of asylum life. Using terms such as *mania* to describe the condition of the physically overactive and the mentally excited patients, and *melancholia* for the inert and depressed, psychiatrists were able to allocate patients to different parts of the wards, so maintaining maximum calm and preventing the more violent patients from aggravating the fears and depressions of others. This in itself was a simple enough consideration, but one which had seldom previously been made.

There was, in fact, a tendency in psychiatry which tried to make the most of the available resources; to make sense simply of what was to be seen in an asylum, and to construct its theories from the observation of the patients themselves. These attitudes go some way to explain the peculiarly lasting influence of the science of physiognomy in psychiatry, for physiognomy was, above all, a science of comparative observation. Based on the assumption of a parallel between the *inner* and the *outer* person, it offered the possibility of diagnosing disease from appearance.

For psychiatrists attempting to study the workings of the mind with only limited resources for their investigations, the prospect of such a method of diagnosis was particularly fascinating, and there were already well-known precedents in general medicine (for example the alterations in a patient's colouring during various diseases of the liver, kidney, intestines etc.). So in the first half of the nineteenth

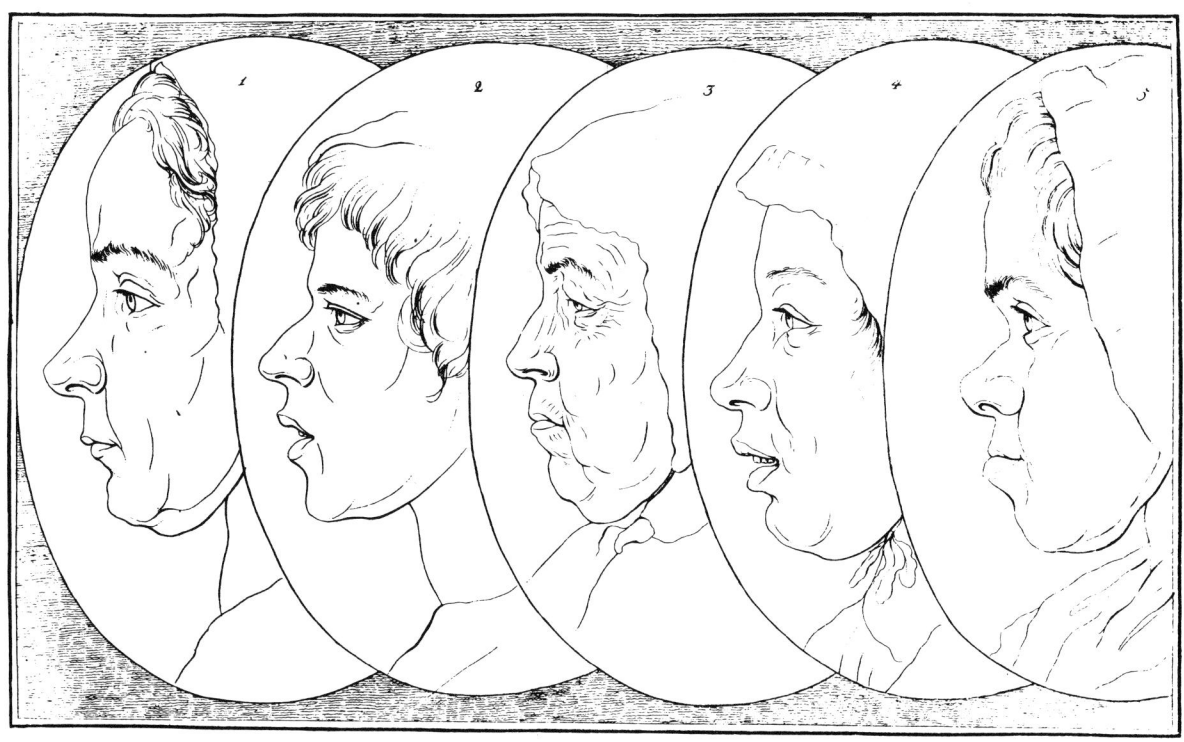

27

Stupidité et Foiblesse d'Esprit (Lavater, 1783)

century a practice had grown up in psychiatry of commissioning artists to portray mental patients for physiognomical research. J.E.D. Esquirol, a pupil of the revolutionary psychiatrist Pinel, and physican to the Salpêtrière in Paris, devoted one section of his comprehensive study of insanity, *Maladies Mentales*, published in 1838, to histories of individual patients in which detailed case-notes are presented with portraits for physiognomical cross-reference. Esquirol's pupil, Georget, commissioned his friend, the artist Gericault, to make portraits of his patients: perhaps the most outstanding results of a painter's work in psychiatry. Among the many psychiatrists who contributed to this research on a more mundane level was the consultant to Springfield and Bethlem in the 1840s, Sir Alexander Morison, whose *Physiognomy of Mental Diseases*, also published in 1838, discusses more than 100 cases using brief notes to supplement the engraved portraits.[5]

So the study which Diamond took up with his patients at Springfield and which formed the basis of Conolly's commentaries to his photographs was an extension of a comparatively well-established tradition in psychiatry. And this tradition had grown up, in an eclectic fashion, to include many apparently contradictory elements: a mixture of three main strands, it drew on the works of Johann Kaspar Lavater, Franz Joseph Gall and Charles Bell.

The study of physiognomy, which dates back to the time of Aristotle, had been revived by the Swiss poet-priest, Lavater, with great popular success in the late eighteenth century. He assembled a vast collection of portraits from which he analysed the faces of the famous and infamous of the past and among his contemporaries, and so succeeded in creating a fashion which lasted well into the nineteenth century.

Working from extremes, 'the man of genius' and 'the idiot born', he tried to trace the characteristic features of different intellectual types by means of comparison, and so began to outline a psychology of character based purely on appearance.[6] Lavater's theories were the product of observation and intuition. Quite uninhibited by a lack of scientific evidence, the sheer imaginative force of his propositions

39

opened up new areas for philosophical specula-tion. Anatomy and physiology were left to future generations – Lavater's concept of physiognomy was a mixture of religion and aesthetics, based on the belief that the soul expressed itself through the form and shape of the body; that like a lamp, it simply shone through the form it inhabited without being physically bound up in it. His theories were dependent not on scientific proof, but on a conviction, a faith in God and in its own validity. This factor enabled Lavater's less scrupulous followers to sidestep physiognomy's core of rigorous aesthetic training, the detailed comparative observation which he himself practised, and to set themselves up as 'face-readers' simply by adopting his conclusions. Physiognomy's credibility as a 'science' declined rapidly. As Conolly pointed out:

> People with odd-shaped eyes looked askance at the disciples of Lavater; and people with long noses or chins disliked having conclusions drawn from them.[7]

Franz Joseph Gall, the originator of phreno-logy (a system for assessing personality from the shape of the skull) had little sympathy with the metaphysical tendencies of Lavater and his fol-lowers. Yet he traced the stimulus for his own research to a childhood physiognomical obser-vation: he had noticed at school that boys with prominent eyes had the best memories. Not content simply to make assertions about such parallels, Gall set out to trace a connection scientifically. A supreme rationalist, he believed that nothing exists in nature, not even man's God-given faculties, without organic support. It was Gall who traced the existence of mechanics for man's higher faculties by locating 'the organ of the soul' – in the human brain.

He too did so by comparative study – comparison between men and animals and the way their abilities vary according to their structure, in particular the structure of the brain. Gall was in fact the first person to recognize the brain as the ultimate complex development of the central nervous system. He wrote:

> By successive additions of new organs, nature progresses step by step and finally reaches up to man only through superposed cerebral productions.[8]

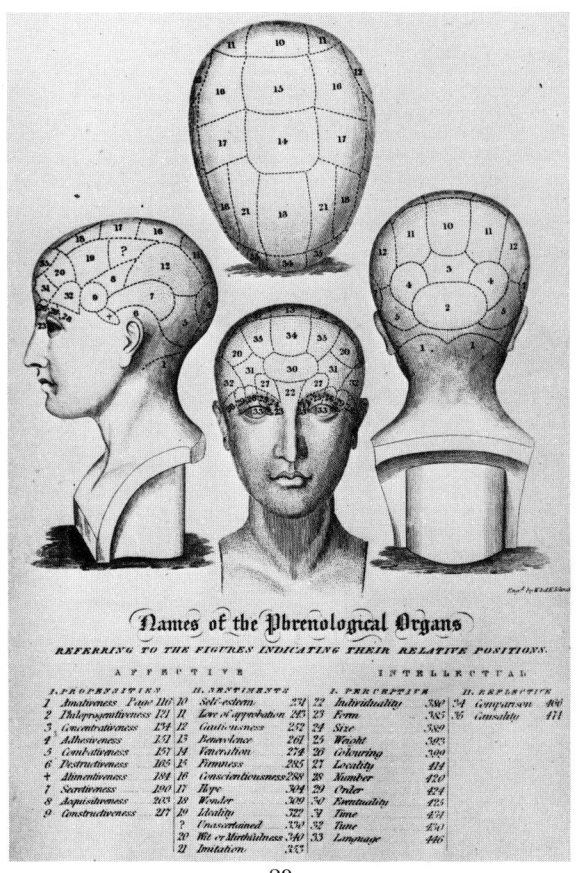

28
Names and Locations of the
Phrenonogical Organs.

Rather than seeing the brain itself as an un-differentiated mass, Gall anatomized it as a system of connected yet individual organs – this in itself constituted a revolution in medical science – and he believed that each of these organs corresponded to a particular faculty or tendency so that hope, self-esteem, language etc. were each dependent on different organic components of the brain. Gall named twenty-seven cerebral organs and believed that their comparative state of development determined a person's abilities – a theory which formed the philosophical basis of the science of phrenology. In an attempt to give his discoveries in the anatomy of the brain an immediate social relevance, Gall followed them through with his own curious mixture of pragmatism and imagi-native logic. His proposition that the skull is moulded on the brain, that a skull's bumps correspond to the size and shape of the various cerebral organs, made the human brain conveniently accessible to examination and led to the idea that psychological make-up could be judged by examining the shape of a skull.

Though the ridicule which has come to surround Gall's phrenological theories has tended to detract from his reputation as an anatomist and obscure the importance of his contribution to modern psychological thought, in the first half of the nineteenth century the implications of his work were still too promising, too immediately relevant for psychiatry, to be eclipsed by phrenology's dubious reputation.

Gall's theories offered psychiatrists logical explanations to questions to which previously there had been no answers. The idea of separate cerebral organs for specific faculties brought up, for example, the question of partial insanity and monomanias implying that these phenomena were the result of malfunction in specific parts of the brain, the rest functioning normally. Such ideas did much to alter the attitudes of psychiatrists towards their patients. They provided a framework within which they began to examine their patients as individuals. Underlying the trappings of 'skull-reading' was a new interest in the precise form taken by each patient's insanity, an interest which assessed personality and took account of behaviour.

For phrenology, though fundamentally concerned with a person's innate qualities, did not treat them as fixed entities. Far from taking a determinist viewpoint, Gall continually stressed the ways in which personality is affected by circumstances of environment – above all education, through which a person could develop and control his or her various faculties and instincts.[9]

Psychiatrists such as Conolly and Diamond responded to this optimistic aspect of phrenology – the dynamic aspect which considered change and looked at people in terms of their potential. When Conolly commented on the configuration of a patient's skull, he did so either to indicate what the patient formerly was, with the idea of restoring full intellectual power; or with regret if this should seem impossible; or with sadness if circumstances had deprived the patient of any opportunity to develop his or her faculties – but never as a way to pass judgement irrevocably on a personality. The emphasis was on the possibility of change, and in the context of insanity, change held out the hope of cure.

The study of such changes called for unusual power of visual discrimination on the part of psychiatrists. And the work of the anatomist, Sir Charles Bell, provided them with a key to the actual workings of the mind which made changes in their patients' mental states accessible to direct observation.

> Of the numerous muscles of the face, all except two which move the lower jaw may be said, says Bell, to be muscles of expression. They arise from some point of the bone, and are inserted in the moveable integuments of the face. Many of them are peculiar to man, and endow him with a much wider range of facial expression than is possessed by any of the lower animals: and commensurate with his superior mental faculties. Some of them contribute also to the movements indispensable to the modulation of his more expressive and varied voice. The large muscle which covers the head from the occiput to the eyebrows, the transverse muscle between the eyebrows, and the circular muscle covering the eyelids, and surrounding the space under the eyes, contribute to the evaluation, and depression, and corrugation of the forehead: movements largely connected with varied expression: and the same muscles close or open the eyes themselves, according as joy, or sorrow, or anger, or other emotion affects the mind. There are separate muscles for raising the soft side portions of the nose, and also the outer angles of the upper lip, and also for depressing them; others for raising the whole upper lip, and for depressing the whole lower lip; and these various actions produce expressions known as indicating gaiety, or melancholy, or contempt, with various modifications.[10]

By tracing the muscular movements accompanying the various emotions and passions, Bell attempted to construct a system for studying the influence of the mind on the body. His *Anatomy of Expression*, examining the mechanics of the mind through the actions of the nervous system on the muscular, moveable parts of the human form, provided a foundation upon which psychiatrists could build their physiognomical practice.[11]

The extracts from Conolly's articles, with his detailed analysis of muscular movements and his emphasis on fluctuations of expression as indicative of changing mental states, give some idea of the value of Bell's work for Victorian psychiatry. And they show how freely physiognomy and phrenology, as fundamental parts of the new discipline of clinical observation, were adapted to the immediate use of psychiatrists. We see Conolly approaching these disciplines with the detachment of experience, selecting, discriminating, avoiding elements of dogma, in order to explore physiognomy's scientific potential. He had seen that physicians trained to observe their patients physiognomically had gained experience which increased their ability to recognize and respond to the signs of mental disorder. He said:

> There may be something of fancy, but there is much more of truth in both of these sciences of observation, some acquaintance with which every one desirous to be an accurate observer ought to possess.[12]

For Dr Diamond, as a photographer of mental patients in the 1850s, the truth of this point had become self-evident. His own interest in physiognomy had begun many years earlier, taking a form reminiscent of Lavater. While researching early printing techniques, he had started to collect engraved portraits of physicians, a physiognomical collection which over the years had grown to include many hundreds of portraits supplemented with biographical notes.[13] His post at Springfield offered an opportunity to extend his physiognomical studies in line with current trends in psychiatry, and by 1856, when Diamond presented the Royal Society with an account of his photographic practice at the Surrey Asylum, he could speak with supreme confidence of 'the well-known sympathy which exists between the diseased brain and the organs and features of the body'.[14] For Diamond, at least, the photographs he exhibited with his paper proved this point beyond a doubt, and in this, his only account of his work as a psychiatrist, it was the use of photography rather than physiognomy which he treated as the novelty requiring explanation.

Point by point Diamond elaborated on the virtues of photography as a method of illustration, giving a new context to that 'unerring accuracy' he had so often praised in photographic journals. Here photography's objectivity, its 'truth', is shown in the way it avoids the 'vague terms' and subjective criteria of verbal descriptions in setting down the data of psychiatry: its precision is seen in the way it quickly records the ever-changing phenomena of human expression. It was, in other words, the ideal method of illustration for studying the physiognomy of insanity. Not only could it record the different phases of an illness with an accuracy no artist could hope to achieve but, now that psychiatrists had begun to study changes in expression as the manifestations of fluctuating mental states, photography could place on record, for the first time ever, the succession of minute variations in expression changing from one moment to the next.

Some series have survived among Diamond's photographs – most of these are 'before and after' portraits: the patient shown while ill and then in convalescence. Some other photographs show patients portrayed in different attitudes at the same sitting. Even so the greater number of photographs are single studies of individual patients – much the same in their intention as many of the previous illustrations made for physiognomical study. But, where painters had been able to depict only the general attitudes and typical expressions of mental patients, photography had minimized the necessity for pre-selection. The almost instantaneous quality of the photograph and the apparently unselective way it responded to detail – qualities with which painters had so often found fault – enabled photographers to record what painters could not. Photographic portraits of mental patients, as Diamond said, are

> ... free altogether from that painful caricaturing which so disfigures almost all the published portraits of the insane as to render them valueless either for purposes of art or of science.[15]

As a photographer discussing the merits of his art, Diamond traces the source of this painful caricaturing to the technical limitations of previous illustrators. One point he does not mention is that most previous illustrations had shown patients in some degree of mechanical restraint. They belonged to the phase in psychiatry which in varying degrees had based its practice on the use of physical coercion. Most patients portrayed from that time experienced the effects of restraints for themselves. If not, they had certainly witnessed them on others.

29
Portrait of a patient before the abolition
of mechanical restraints, 1838

30
'Madness', 1806 (*Bell*)

Fifty years before Diamond made his photographs, Sir Charles Bell, one of the earliest illustrators of mental patients for medico-physiognomical study, paid a visit to Bethlem Hospital to make an illustration of 'Madness' for his *Anatomy of Expression*. He found, to his surprise, that a constant element in the expression of the 'outrageous maniac' was fear.[16] Only after the abolition of restraints could his observation be fully understood. Conolly wrote:

> In those times, the galleries and cells of asylums presented vivid expressions of malady to the artist: such as now will be looked for in vain. It was not simple malady indeed which was generally depicted in the faces of the wretched people who then raved or moped in such places: but malady aggravated by mechanical coercion, or by neglect, or by positive cruelty.[17]

The illustrations of mental patients from this period had, unwittingly, recorded the results of methods used in asylums rather than the physiognomy of insanity.

By the 1850s Bell's version of the madman had disappeared from the wards of public asylums. The abolition of restraints had brought unexpectedly direct changes in the very appearance of 'madness'. Psychiatrists like Diamond, in daily contact with these results for years on end, had come almost to take them for granted. What they saw corresponded with their changed attitude towards insanity. But what of the general public?

In 1856 J.C. Bucknill, Superintendent of the Devon County Asylum, described the disappointment of a Shakespearean actor who had visited the asylum to study the patients. 'Where is the poetry of madness?' the actor asked. 'I see none of it, no flashing eye, no foam on the mouth. Why, your people are as sober and as respectable as a vestry meeting!' Bucknill had tried to explain that since mental patients had been treated 'on rational and human principles', they no longer offered 'the best and most constant examples of exaggerated passion'.[18]

Dr Diamond brought the 'physiognomy' of asylum reforms out to the public by exhibiting his photographs. They could have shown, once

43

and for all, that the concept of the 'outrageous lunatic' belonged to the past, but it was not so easy to replace the old images of madness in the public eye. Exhibited without any explanatory notes to people who were not necessarily intent on reading faces or tracing expression, the photographs were not as instantly informative as Diamond suggests. He exhibited them as 'Types of Insanity' or 'Portraits of Insane Persons', and the very word *insanity*, as the reviews show, was too evocative, too weighted with its own history to allow Diamond's portraits to speak for themselves and demonstrate the contrast between old and new. Though his images of patients challenged old accepted notions of insanity, the challenge went unnoticed, and the critical blindness which assigned Diamond's portraits to a place alongside Hogarth and Kaulbach amounts to an unwitting, passive perpetuation of the past. The public, it seems, simply could not see what it did not understand.

As a psychiatrist, Diamond chose to speak through the images he made. He rarely supplied any commentary to his photographs to offer hints as to how they should be approached or to give interpretations of what they depicted. His method was uncompromisingly visual.

In his only written account of his work, his emphasis is on its practical rather than theoretical aspects, on what happened in the asylum studio. There is a tendency to quote the observations and opinions of other psychiatrists on theoretical matters. His own voice is heard in stories of asylum life. It is here that Diamond had made his personal contribution to Victorian psychiatry. When he began his photographic study of the physiognomy of insanity he certainly had not foreseen exactly what the outcome would be and to what extent the patients themselves were to become involved with his project. He said:

> . . . I may refer with pleasure to a case in which photography unquestionably led to the cure. A.D., aged 20 was admitted under my care in August, 1854, having been recently discharged uncured from the Bethlem Hospital after a year's residence there. Her delusions consisted in the supposed possession of great wealth, and of an exalted station as a queen. Any occupation was therefore looked upon by her as below her dignity. I wished to possess portraits of several

> patients who imagined themselves to be Queens and Royal Personages . . . It was however not without much persuasion that I induced the Queen, A.D., to give me the honour of a sitting. I told her that it was my wish to take portraits of all the Queens under my care, and well I remember the contempt with which she observed 'Queens indeed! How did they obtain their titles?' I replied: as she did, *they imagined them*. 'No,' she said sharply. 'I never imagine such foolish delusions, they are to be pitied, but I was born a Queen.' Her subsequent amusement at seeing the portraits and her frequent conversation about them was the first decided step in her gradual improvement, and about four months ago she was discharged and laughed heartily at her former imaginations.[19]

Diamond's account of this case is remarkably informal – an amusing anecdote from the asylum ward almost entirely taken up with the conversation between himself and A.D. about his photographic project and her position as a Queen. So where did the photographic cure come from? Not directly from studying the physiognomy of insanity. The cure came, according to Diamond, not from anything he discovered from the portrait which enabled him to direct her treatment. It came from what the Queen took from these photographic activities for herself.

It would obviously be stretching the point too far to deduce from this one story, with its reference to 'frequent conversations' about the photographs, that Diamond conducted formal therapy sessions with his patients to discuss their portraits. Certainly Diamond never mentioned such a practice. His emphasis is on the advantages of photography as a source of interest for the patients, one which had the additional advantage of drawing their attention to their own condition.[20] This interest had been the first step towards recovery in the case of A.D. and in many other cases Diamond had found that the mental stimulus photography provided had brought beneficial results.

The picture we are given of photographic sessions is of a shared activity, a focusing point for conversation where interest went hand in hand with entertainment. Diamond valued photography for the entertainment it gave. He had introduced it into asylum life in the pursuit of scientific truth, only to discover a more immediate source of benefit to the patients: that entertainment itself was a valid psychiatric tool.

By 1858, Conolly could write:

. . . the taking of portraits has become one of the pleasures of which the patients cheerfully partake in our lunatic asylums; and helps, in combination with the various other alleviations studied by humane superintendents, to diversify and cheer the days passed in necessary seclusion from the busier, but scarcely happier world, with-out.[21]

Other psychiatrists had in fact followed Diamond's example and taken up photography.[22] They had done so at a time when psychiatrists were becoming increasingly aware of the therapeutic value of entertainments for their patients. Numerous examples can be found in contemporary asylum reports. One tells of how the introduction of cricket matches into asylum activities by the Resident Physician had led to the recovery of several patients, among them a suicidal baker 'who could not be induced to occupy himself in any way until his mental and physical energies were aroused by this game'.[23] Another story, from the Lunatic Department of the Naval Hospital at Haslar, tells of fishing excursions at sea:

In the first of these little voyages a patient, whose voice had not been heard for years, was so delighted with his success that he counted his fish aloud.[24]

One impression that such stories give is of the individuality of the various asylums, the way that in spite of any bureaucratic interventions they reflect the ideas of their psychiatrists. Perhaps it was simply that scientific methods had not then become so formalized as to exclude apparently fanciful experiments – such scientifically questionable yet artistically entertaining projects as for example, photographing 'all the Queens' in an asylum. The unforeseen 'result' of this particular project, the *cure* of A.D., is typical of the experimental nature of non-restraint psychiatry.

There must too have been a considerable fluidity in any institutional set-up which as early as the 1850s included fishing expeditions as part of its activities, or allowed Diamond to incorporate his personal interests into his work and share them with his patients. In these early years of the asylum era, there was still a degree of spontaneity about the introduction of such entertainments. The fact that psychiatrists often lived in the asylums, that, as in the case of Diamond and his photographic studio, a part of their private lives took place within the asylum walls, must have made it more probable, even though not inevitable, that an extra-medical relationship should grow up between psychiatrist and patient. The definition of the psychiatrist's role within these institutions still had not separated responsibility for *entertaining* from that of *caring* and allocated it to a department of its own. Before the days when entertainment came to be institutionalized, some psychiatrists seem to have had considerable success informally as occupational therapists.

Yet photography never took on an aspect of pure benevolence for Diamond, making it simply an entertainment to be dispensed to patients. There was nothing patronizing about his portrait-making and no signs of an attempt simply to please can be traced in the images he produced. His discovery of the effects of photography on the patients themselves only added to the complexity of an activity in which personal, artistic and scientific motives seem to have remained constant. His photographic practice at Springfield depended on shared interest and joint participation and the quality of the photographs as portraits derives from that balance of interests he was able to establish with his patients under the non-restraint system.

Something of all this – of these many strands of experiment – has found expression in all the photographs presented here, from Springfield and from Bethlem. They belong so completely to the non-restraint era of the 1850s precisely because of their complexity: the many interacting ways they have simultaneously recorded and contributed to asylum psychiatry.

Although made in institutions at a time when the administrative use of photographs was coming to be recognized, they are devoid of those impersonal qualities – the brutal uniformity of pose and format – already found in the photographs made for police and prison records in the 1850s[25] and which were to appear later in asylum photographs made towards the end of the century. As illustrations of the physiognomy of mental disease they do not show the clinical detachment of later medical photographs, many of which record only isolated

31
Portrait of a friend: The Rev. J.R. Major, *c.* 1856 (*Diamond*)

32

Portrait of a patient, *c.* 1855 (*Diamond*)

details of a patient – specific physical signs of malfunction. All these 'portraits of the insane' were made to illustrate a more general belief: that mental states affect a person's appearance and therefore can be judged from it. This attitude, finding importance in the slightest gesture or detail of dress, in the way patients presented themselves and responded to others, looked to record as many facets as possible of a patient's appearance. It was an attitude which allowed the patient an unprecedented freedom of expression, for the authenticity and validity of the psychiatrist's observations depended on it.

So too did the taking of photographs. Cooperation was essential. As long as the technical limitations of photography called for formal sittings there could still be no action photographs, no scenes snapped in the ward, no secret portraits taken while a patient was

33
Dr Diamond aged 65

unaware. Each patient in these portraits – whether in Dr Diamond's studio at the Surrey Asylum or in the more limited environment of the wards of Bethlem Hospital (more limited in the case of those portraits from Bethlem's 'Criminal Lunatic' department, where patients would not have been allowed to leave their wards) – each of these patients has agreed to sit quite still for an exposure time of several seconds. Yet none of them betray the constrained look of a figure posed by a photographer.

Conolly tells us that one patient at Bethlem who disliked her dress would only agree to sit for her portrait if she were shown reading a book. The patient read her book, though upside down, and the portrait was made. Each portrait in a varying degree is the result of such an agreement between psychiatrist, photographer and patient, the terms worked out together. Pointless to speculate on how much was decided by each, but certainly the way in which the

photographs were made as medical illustrations well over a hundred years ago gives them their impact as portraits today. Very few portraits exist of people in such extreme mental states photographed with such calm formality. Very few such formal photographs retain such a degree of personal sympathy. The very ease with which the patients pose for their portraits testifies to an unusually relaxed relationship between patient and psychiatrist, photographer and sitter and tells us something of the quality of non-restraint psychiatry practised in the 1850s.

The woman in the checked dress sits, smiling, holding a pigeon in her lap; the old man looks sideways into the distance; another woman, hands held together, lips apart, looks straight out at us. Some appear preoccupied while others enter into the event with visible enjoyment. But not one is simply resigned to having a picture taken. Despite the formality of sittings the faces have not frozen – and with astonishing directness each person confronts the camera.

Notes

Introduction (pp.1-5)

1. 'From today painting is dead': The Beginnings of Photography. An exhibition presented by the Arts Council of Great Britain at the Victoria and Albert Museum, 16 March–14 May 1972.
2. The portraits were listed in the catalogue as 'Six photographs of mental patients'. Also exhibited was 'The Göschenen entrance to the St. Gotthard Tunnel, 1872', by Dr Diamond.
3. The albums were begun at the suggestion of Henry G. Wright, MD. 'Dr Wright was a photographer of no mean order. His contributions to pathological photography were numerous and excellent, and he inaugurated the effort of the Medical and Chirurgical Society to form a collection of photographs of medical and surgical cases of interest. This proposition was carried into effect in 1862, under his own superintendence, and he lavished a fatherly care upon the two large albums containing the collection, and the case book containing the records of the cases' (*Lancet*, 23 January 1869).
4. Thirteen articles on 'The Physiognomy of Insanity' by John Conolly, MD, published in the *Medical Times and Gazette* between January 1858 and February 1859.
5. John Conolly, *The Treatment of the Insane without Mechanical Restraints*, 1856. Reprint: R. Hunter & I. Macalpine, Dawsons, London 1973 (p. 53).
6. The parcel containing the original mounted photographs was labelled 'Parcel of photographs of patients taken under Sir Charles Hood (1852-62). Presented by his granddaughter. 42 photographs mounted. Note of their origin unsigned.'

   A separate parcel contained 59 unmounted photographs, later prints, mainly duplicates of the mounted series. A smaller collection of the original glass negatives was also subsequently found in the hospital archives. No mention of these prints or negatives has been found in the hospital records of that period.
7. Henry Hering, a printseller at 137 Regent's Street from 1851, first appears on the records as a photographer in 1857. Little other information is so far available about him.

   Of the eleven cases discussed by Conolly in these articles, two were illustrated with engravings from photographs in the Bethlem collection and nine from Springfield. Under one of the engravings from the Bethlem series is the caption 'from a photograph by Dr Diamond'. The other Bethlem illustrations are not credited. All the engravings from the Springfield photographs are given as Diamond's work except for the final engraving which is not credited. No mention is made of Hering in the articles. Diamond is the only photographer named, though the fact that other psychiatrists had followed his example is mentioned several times (see also Part 3, note 22).

   The fact that more than half the mounted series of Bethlem photos are credited 'Hering photo' (mainly in pencil on the mounts) is now considered to outweigh the attribution to Diamond in the *Medical Times & Gazette*, which must therefore be seen as an error.
8. *Athenaeum*, 3 July 1886.
9. I.C. Lodge Patch, 'Treatment or Punishment? A Nineteenth-century Scandal', *Journal of Psychological Medicine*, 6, 143-9.
10. House of Commons Papers (1857) no. 77,14, no. 77, 199-268.
11. On the other hand Dr Diamond has been widely credited with the introduction of the *carte-de-visite*. See Helmut Gernsheim, *The History of Photography*, Thames & Hudson,

London, 1969 (p. 224). For Diamond's own account, see *The Year Book of Photography & Photographic News Almanac*, London, 1880 (p. 29): 'I have now on a table some of the little pictures, some of which Her Majesty did me the honour to accept through Dr Becker's attention, and which led to the introduction of the *carte-de-visite*.'

12. Dr Diamond exhibited his photographs under the following titles:

> 'Types of Insanity' (1852)
> 'Phases of the Insane'(1854)
> 'Portraits of Insane Persons'(1856)
> 'Studies of Insane Persons'(1857)
> 'Illustrations of Mental Disease'(1859)

In the catalogue of the 1854 Exhibition of the Photographic Society the following note was added to the title 'Phases of the Insane': 'These portraits of the insane are intended to show some of the various peculiar physiognomical characters of the affliction, and the four lower exhibit the same case in different stages, melancholy, excited, convalescent and well.'

13. The contents of Twickenham House were auctioned on 16, 17 and 18 June 1887. In the catalogue, lots 550-8 were listed as 'Albums & portfolios', Lot 700 as 'Cameras etc.'.

14. Dr Diamond, 'On the Application of Photography to the Physiognomic and Mental Phenomena of Insanity', Royal Society, 1856 (see below, p. 153).

1 Dr Hugh Welch Diamond (pp.6-21)

1. William Bachelor Diamond (1786-1855) was granted a licence to open an asylum by the Royal College of Physicians on 19 October 1820. His asylum, Weston House, stood on the site now occupied by St Pancras Station. In 1847 he moved to Henley-in-Arden, where he was joint licensee, with a Dr Burman, of Burman House Lunatic Asylum, until his death in 1855.

2. Warren Hastings Diamond (1835-1910). In 1858 he became Resident Superintendent of Effra Hall, Brixton, described in an advertisement in the *Medical Directory* as being 'for the care and recovery of nervous, epileptic and insane ladies'.

3. See 'Medicine, the City, and China', by Denis Leigh, *Medical History*, Vol.18, No. 1, 1974. For full details of the voyages of W.B. Diamond see *Hardy's Register of Ships*, 1760-1833, Vol.1.

4. 'Diamond, William Bachelor, and Welch, Jane Jarvis, Spinster and a Minor by licence (with the consent of her mother)' (Parish Register, Goudhurst, Kent, 5 January 1808).

5. 'He suffered five separate attacks: the first in 1765 at the age of 27 which was hushed up, relapses in 1801 and 1804, and the final breakdown in 1810 when 72 years old which resulted in the establishment of the Regency and lasted to his death in 1820. But the best documented and most important not only for the political issues it raised but also for the stimulus it gave to psychiatry was the second attack from October 1788 until March 1789. The physicians who attended him were repeatedly summoned before Parliamentary Committees to depose about "the state of His Majesty's health" when they were questioned about their royal patient's illness in the light of their practical experience of insanity. These reports were frequently reprinted in popular or "cheap" editions' (R. Hunter & I. Macalpine: *Three Hundred Years of Psychiatry, 1535-1860*, Oxford University Press, London, 1963).

For a full account of these events, see *George III and the Mad-Business*, by the same authors, A.Lane, London, 1969.

6. It would appear from an obituary in the *Gentleman's Magazine*, November 1855, that W.B. Diamond had already taken up the special study of mental disorders while still living in Sussex.

7. See Dr Diamond's obituary in the *Athenaeum*, 3 July 1886: 'An entry in one of the parish registers of Brenchley, Co. Kent, certifies that John Dimont, son of John Dimonte the Frenchman, was buried there on the 17th of November, 1638. As workers in iron, some of these Kentish Diamonds were at one time employed on iron-work for St Paul's Cathedral.'

8. The Apothecaries Act of 1815 laid down the first regulations for examining medical practitioners, appointing the Society of Apothecaries to 'superintend the execution and provisions of this act'. 'No person was admitted to examination unless he was 21 years of age, had "served an apprenticeship of not less than five years to an apothecary" and produced testimonials of a "sufficient medical education, and of good moral conduct" – from that time only those already in practice and "properly certified new entrants" could practise as apothecaries in England and Wales.'

Hugh Welch Diamond was certified to practise as an apothecary on 26 November 1829. The following regulations for medical practitioners had been introduced in 1827:

1. He must have served an apprenticeship of not less than five years, and must be of the full age of 21 and of good moral character.

2. He must produce certificates that he had attended not less than one course of lectures in a) *Materia Medica* and Medical Botany; b) Chemistry; c) two courses of lectures in Anatomy and Physiology; d) two courses of lectures in the

Theory and Practice of Medicine, and these must have been attended subsequent to the lectures on *Materia Medica*, Medical Botany, and Chemistry.

'The certificates for the lectures on the Principles and Practice of Medicine required the signature of a "Fellow Candidate, or Licentiate of the Royal College of Physicians".

A certificate was also required that the candidate had attended for at least six months the medical practice of some public Hospital or Infirmary, or for nine months at a Dispensary, and that such attendance commenced subsequent to the termination of the first course of lectures on the Principles and Practice of Medicine.

'Candidates were also recommended to attend one or more courses of lectures on Midwifery and the Diseases of Women and Children.

'The precise subjects in which papers were set were: 1) Translating grammatically parts of the *pharmacopoeia Londinensis* and Physician's Prescriptions; 2) Chemistry; 3) *Materia Medica* and Medical Botany; 4) Anatomy and Physiology; 5) The Practice of Medicine' (W.S.C. Copeman, *The Worshipful Society of Apothecaries of London: A History 1617–1967*, Oxford, Pergamon Press, 1967).

9. 'The intention of the proposed Dispensary is "to prescribe for, and supply the Sick Poor of Maidstone and its vicinity, with Medicines gratuitously, to promote Vaccination, and also to furnish the ruptured Poor with Trusses at reduced prices".

'The industrious and independent Poor; by the independent Poor are meant those who do not receive Parochial relief; will, through this Charity, receive gratuitous advice and medicines, and thus be assisted in supporting themselves and families, without applying to a Parish, or involving themselves in debt to their Medical Attendant, with little, or no prospect of ever being able to pay him. Those also, who, through unavoidable misfortunes, have fallen into poverty, and are unable to pay for the attendance of a Medical Gentleman, and feel unwilling to apply for Parochial Assistance, will find great comfort from the eleemosynary aid of this Institution.

'Those who receive relief from a Parish are, by the same means, supplied with proper Medical attendance; and are not, therefore, *generally*, to be considered proper objects of this Charity; they are not, however, excluded, when the opinion of a Physician may be desirable; if recommended by a 'Governor' (Extract from the *Plan of the Maidstone Dispensary*, 1830).

10. *The Times*, 17 March 1832.

11. 'The Case of Mrs. Catherine Cummings', *Journal of Psychological Medicine and Mental Pathology*, Vol. 5, 1852.

12. R. Derek Wood, 'J.B. Reade and the Early History of Photography', *Annals of Science*, Vol. 27, March 1971.

13. Ibid. See also R. Derek Wood, 'The Rev. J.B. Reade' (and Dr Hugh Diamond's earliest photography), *British Journal of Photography*, Vol. 119, July 1972.

14. *Archaeologia*, Vol. 27, 1836 (p. 405). Hugh Welch Diamond had been made a Fellow of the Society of Antiquaries in 1834.

15. *Archaeologia*, Vol. 30, 1846 (p. 408).

16. Charles Roach-Smith: *Retrospections*, 1883.

17. Jehangeer Nowrojee and Hirjeebhoy Merwanjee, of Bombay: *Journal of a Residence of Two and a Half Years in Great Britain*, Allen & Co., London, 1841.

18. *Athenaeum*, 3 July 1886.

19. For Diamond's account of these excavations see *Archaeologia*, Vol. 32, 1847.

20. In March 1850, shortly after moving to the asylum, Diamond's wife Jane Warwick (daughter of Mark Warwick of Cumberland), died of a 'fever' while in premature labour. She left Diamond three children: Warren Hastings, Mary Margaret and Hugh Ernest. In April of the following year, Diamond married a twenty-five-year-old widow, Teresa Butler.

21. In his 'Report on Photographic Proof and Apparatus' as a juror for the Paris Exhibition of 1867, Dr Diamond wrote:
'Though Mr Archer gave this beautiful process, in its very perfect state, to the public in 1851, it must not be supposed that he had arrived at its good results without great research and numberless experiments, for it can be verified beyond all doubt that in November 1847, he was taking calotype pictures, and applying substances in the open air to improve the surface of the paper. By slow gradations these early experiments culminated in the process given to his friends in 1850, and published in the *Chemist* in 1851.'

22. 'Photography applied to the Microscope etc.' (*Notes & Queries*, First Series, Vol. VI, No. 163, December 1852).

23. On the subject of photography, the Editor, W.J. Thoms, had this to say: 'By means of photography, a few pounds, combined with some small experience, would enable each county historian to be his own artist, and the printer of the views which he has himself taken; for it must be remembered that photographic sketches may be multiplied by printing with very little trouble' (*Notes & Queries*, First Series, Vol. VI, No. 148, August 1852).

24. *Notes & Queries*, First Series, Vol. VII, No. 166, January 1853.

25. 'Southey came over to spend the day in photography, but we went instead to Dr Diamond of the Surrey Lunatic Asylum. He gave me two he had done lately – an excellent full-length of Uncle Skeffington, and a boy at King's College, Frank Forester' (Roger Lancelyn Green (ed), *The Diaries of Lewis Carroll*, Cassell, London, 1953).

26. See illustration 10.

27. Dr Diamond was appointed Honorary Photographer to the Society of Antiquaries in February 1854.

28. 'The Art of Photography is at length taking its place beside that of engraving in the publication of Portraits. We have several specimens before us. Dr Diamond has been induced to issue some of his 'Portraits of the Men of the Time'; and we doubt not many an old King's College man will be glad to have an opportunity of securing the admirable likeness which Dr Diamond has produced of the Rev. Dr Major, the learned and excellent master of King's College School; while the many friends who appreciate the literary acquirements and social character of the author of the Handbook of London, will be no less delighted with the genial and characteristic likeness of Mr Peter Cunningham, which Dr Diamond has succeeded in catching. These are separate publications' (*Notes & Queries*, Second Series, Vol. II, No. 27, July 1856).

29. This advertisement appeared in *Notes & Queries*, First Series, Vol. X, No. 266, December 1854. Also in the *Asylum Journal of Mental Science*, February 1855.

30. For a full account of Fox Talbot's patent restrictions, see Helmut Gernsheim, *The History of Photography*, Thames & Hudson, London 1969.

Fox Talbot himself wrote the following letter to Dr Diamond:
Dear Sir,
I received a communication some time ago to which I have hitherto omitted to reply, simply from want of time and continual occupation, but as perhaps my silence may be liable to misconstruction I will trouble you with a few lines of explanation.

I was asked in a printed circular to submit towards a testimonial to be presented to you as the author of improvements in Photography as applied to Archaeology. Had it been proposed on the ground of your admirable success in applying photography to the Portraiture of Insanity I should have been most happy to have added my name. And the simple fact is that I was not aware you had applied the art to Archaeology and that I have laid down a rule to myself never to add my name as testifying to anything which I cannot really vouch for to a certain extent at least.

H.F. Talbot
About twelve or fourteen years ago I made a great number of Specimens connected with Archaeology and Philology (inscriptions etc.) some of which I could find and should be happy to send you some' (Reproduced by courtesy of the Wellcome Trustees).

31. See Dr Diamond's paper to the Royal Society: 'On the Application of Photography to the Physiognomic and Mental Phenomena of Insanity'.

32. *The Times*, 31 December 1852.

33. *Journal of the Society of Arts*, 31 December 1852.

34. *Athenaeum*, January 1853.

35. Alison Gernsheim, 'Medical Photography in the Nineteenth Century', *Medical and Biological Illustration*, Vol.XI, No. 2, April 1961.

36. *Athenaeum*, January 1853.

37. John Leighton: 'On Photography as a Means or an End', *The Builder*, 1 October 1853.

38. Ibid.

39. *Athenaeum*, January 1854.

40. Ibid.

41. *The Builder*, January 1854.

42. Ernest Lacan and A. Gaudin, *Esquisses Photographiques à propos de l'exposition universelle et de la guerre d'orient*, Paris 1856.

43. E. Lacan: ibid. (pp. 75–6).

44. E. Lacan: ibid. (p. 76).

45. *Athenaeum*, 10 January 1857.

46. *Saturday Review*, 24 January 1857.

47. *Photographic Journal*, 26 February 1857.

48. *Photographic News*, 4 February 1859.

49. *Richmond and Twickenham Times*, 26 June 1886.

50. As early as 3 March 1854, the following notice appeared in the *Asylum Journal of Mental Science*: 'Physiognomy of Insanity*: A series of Photographic Portraits from the life, by Dr Hugh W. Diamond, FSA. With Brief Medical Notes. To be published in occasional parts, small quarto.'

This advertisement appeared again in the next issue, but no further mention of the project was made. It would seem that the publication never appeared – certainly no photographic or medical historian has ever found a copy. It has been suggested that this material was simply transferred to Conolly as the basis for his articles in the *Medical Times and Gazette*.

51. The following entry appeared in the *Photographic Journal* on 16 February 1869:

'Sonnet to Dr Diamond, on his retiring from the Secretaryship of the London Photographic Society.

The tranquil shades of evening close around;
Twilight lingers as the day expires;
So worthy Diamond from his post retires,
As mellow leaves glide gently to the ground.

Withdrawn and gone have been some more
    renown'd –
More fervid with their hidden fires –
More daring in their bold desires –
But none more modest, more profound.
The aid he gave his favourite art aright
He never told; it never will be known.
Within the inner circle *there* he shone,
And, diamond-like, diffused his brilliant light.
Can worth than this obtain a truer test? –
Who know him most are those who love him best.

                        H.J.

52.   *Photographic Journal*, 15 December 1862.

2 The Case of Daniel Dolley (pp. 22-34)

1.   House of Commons Papers (1857), No. 77, 14, no. 77. Communications Respecting the Medical Superintendent of the Surrey Lunatic Asylum, (p. 67).

2.   'The two Acts of Parliament of 1845 "for the Regulation and Treatment of Lunatics" (8 & 9 Vict., c 100) and "to amend the Laws for the Provision and Regulation of Lunatic Asylums for Counties and Boroughs, and for the Maintenance and Care of Pauper Lunatics" (8 & 9 Vict., c 126) resulted from the *Report* of 1844 and were, like it, the work of Lord Shaftesbury. The new Commissioners in Lunacy (five laymen, three physicians and three barristers-at-law) constituted a permanent centralized full-time body with Lord Shaftesbury as Chairman, to supervise all that pertained to the insane throughout the land by inspecting, licensing and reporting to Parliament. They were to inspect asylums annually, provisional licensed houses twice yearly and metropolitan houses four times a year (excepting only Bethlem Hospital which remained exempt until 1853, the clause in the bill bringing it within the commissioners' purview having been expunged by the House of Lords); they were empowered to visit gaols, workhouses or any institution where insane persons were confined. For ease of inspection all asylums were required to keep "Registers and Medical Records . . . in a specified and uniform shape"' (R.A. Hunter & I. Macalpine: *Three Hundred Years of Psychiatry, 1535–1860*, Oxford University Press, London, 1963, p. 995).

3.   Ibid.

4.   The Retreat was opened in June 1796. See Samuel Tuke, *Description of the Retreat, an Institution Near York, for Insane Persons of the Society of Friends*, Alexander, York, 1815.

5.   In the Further Report of the Commissioners in Lunacy to the Lord Chancellor, June 1847, the following account is given of conditions in the York Asylum in the year 1815 when public demand had finally led to an official inquiry: 'It was found, at that time, that there were concealed rooms in the Hospital, unknown even to the Governors of the Asylum; and that patients slept in these rooms, which were saturated with filth, and totally unfit for the habitation of any human being. Thirteen female patients were crowded in a room twelve feet by seven feet ten inches only; the keepers had access to the female wards and several female patients became pregnant. One patient (a clergyman) was kicked downstairs by a keeper, whilst his wife was insulted by the keepers with indecent language, in order to deter her from visiting him. Another male patient disappeared, and was never afterwards heard of; four patients were supposed to be burned to death (the Asylum having been "found to be on fire", a few days after a general investigation of it was directed); and there were several other patients "of whom no account could be given".'

6.   See illustration 20. 'The enormities existing in Asylums, public as well as private, previously to the Parliamentary investigations of 1815, 1816 and 1827, can scarcely be exaggerated. They comprise almost every species of cruelty, insult and neglect, to which helpless and friendless people can be exposed, when abandoned to the charge of ignorant, idle, and ferocious keepers, acting without conscience or control' (Further Report of the Commissioners in Lunacy to the Lord Chancellor, June 1847).

7.   For Conolly's account of the non-restraint system and the changes made at Hanwell, see John Conolly, *The Treatment of the Insane without Mechanical Restraints*, 1856. Reprint: R. Hunter & I. Macalpine, Dawsons, London, 1973.

8.   Commissioners in Lunacy (1854) Eighth Report to the Lord Chancellor, Appendix (B) (p. 140), House of Commons, London.

9.   It would seem that the problems of the asylum had begun on the drawing-board: 'It was the design of the architect that the Asylum should be warmed by steam and for this purpose cast-iron steam pipes, four inches in diameter, were laid down under the flooring of every part of the building, at the cost under the original contract of more than 2,000 pounds. These pipes were not of sufficient strength to bear the pressure to which they had to be exposed; they consequently burst very frequently, sometimes with great violence. During the first two winters after the Asylum was opened, engineers, bricklayers, and carpenters were almost constantly employed in repairing injuries done in this manner both to the pipes and to the building . . . On opening the Asylum it was found that the construction of nearly all the

windows was imperfect, and that the ventilation of the Establishment was far from being satisfactory. These evils were remedied by the introduction of a large number of new cast-iron window frames, on an improved principle, and by the insertion of more than 1,100 copper ventilating casements in the various windows throughout the Asylum' (Surrey County Lunatic Asylum [1843] Annual Report).

10. Ibid.

11. 'The Committee have also reason to believe that since the Asylum has been opened, and the advantages it afforded to lunatics have become known and recognized throughout the County, many poor insane persons, long previously neglected at home, have been brought under the notice of the parish officers and readily acknowledged to be suitable for admission to the Asylum . . .' (Surrey County Lunatic Asylum [1850] Special Report for the Erection of Additional Buildings at Springfield).

12. 'A building covering nearly seven acres of ground, and containing as does the Surrey Asylum, 1,022 windows, 619 doors, 163 fire-places, 38 cisterns, 25 baths, 270 water taps and stop cocks, 307 gas-burners, with an extensive apparatus for cooking, and washing and drying linen, in which nearly forty thousand gallons of hot and cold water are distributed daily by steam power through more than 4,000 yards of lead piping, can be kept in repair only at great expense, especially when it is considered that it is occupied by nearly 800 persons most of whom being patients, act generally without judgement, and sometimes with violence . . . The Committee are ready to allow very cheerfully everything that may be necessary for the recovery of the patients, as well as a large amount of indulgences; but a due regard to the patients themselves, whose position in life is of the humblest kind, as well as to the ratepayers of the County by whom the Asylum is maintained, renders it imperative on the Committee to require that the latter be of an inexpensive kind, and that the Asylum be conducted as economically as possible' (Surrey County Lunatic Asylum [1858] Annual Report).

13. In his annual report to the Committee of Visitors for the year 1853, Dr Diamond writes: 'I also beg to call the attention of the Committee to the extremely trivial circumstances which induce the Work house authorities to return patients here. It frequently happens that an inmate who is a little troublesome in the Workhouse is threatened to be sent back to the Asylum. This not only irritates the persons, but they, knowing themselves to be more comfortable here than in the Union House, by their own conduct favour their own removal. They are often returned to us as sane in their minds as at the time of their discharge. They conform to our rules and give us no trouble whatever. This also takes place frequently when there is a wish to transfer a patient from the charge of the parish to that of the County . . . I fear, however, a disposition exists to send here a great number of quite hopeless cases, neither dangerous to themselves or others. Such cases, I think, the parishes should retain in their own workhouses, as they are quite harmless and require merely the attention of an ordinary nurse. The admission of such cases, when there is ample accommodation in the Asylum, is unobjectionable; but it is very desirable that such admissions should be so limited as never to prevent the admission of curable cases, suffering from acute mania, and consequently requiring that full prompt medical relief so readily afforded in establishments of this kind, but so difficult to be obtained elsewhere . . .'

14. For the full text of the evidence heard at this inquiry see House of Commons Papers (1857) No. 77, 14, no. 77, Communications Respecting the Medical Superintendent of the Surrey Lunatic Asylum (pp. 10–22). .

15. Ibid. (p. 23).

16. Ibid. (p. 53).

17. Ibid. (pp. 29–36).

18. 'An investigation before Mr Henry, at Bow Street, has shown the utility of the Lunacy Commission. That body has decided a prosecution against the resident surgeon of the Wandsworth asylum, on the charge of having occasioned the death of an elderly lunatic, by a means which excited a horror akin to that with which one reads the records of Fox, touching the martyrs to that missionary institution known as the Inquisition' (*Illustrated London News*. Quoted in the *Asylum Journal of Mental Science*, 1856, 2, 517–23).

19. Ibid.

20. House of Commons Papers (1857) No. 77, 14, no. 77, Communications Respecting the Medical Superintendent of the Surrey Lunatic Asylum (pp. 36–8), from which the following extracts of the prosecution brief are also taken:

W. Charles Hood MD (Resident Medical Superintendent of Bethlem Hospital): '. . . that it is witness's firm belief that he never witnessed a shower-bath given for more than three minutes, and his strong impression is that he never knew one given for so long a period; that in regard to Dolley's case, it is witness's opinion that he died from the effect of the long-continued cold-water shower-bath, followed by the dose of tartar emetic'.

Henry Stevens MD (Resident Medical Super

intendent, St Luke's Hospital): '. . . that witness does not consider that the administering of a shower-bath for 28 minutes to an insane person of 65 years of age can be properly designated medical treatment; that witness would expect that the subjecting of a patient of 65 years of age to a cold-water shower-bath for a period of 28 minutes, followed by a dose of tartar emetic, would terminate fatally'.

Wm. Lawrence, Esq (Senior Surgeon to St Bartholomew's Hospital): '. . . as a matter of opinion, witness thinks such treatment would be likely to kill any man of 65 years of age, whether sane or insane, and witness is of opinion, that in the present case the death of the patient was occasioned by the long-continued shower-bath, followed by the dose of tartar emetic. Indeed, the witness's expression to us was, that he thought the shower-bath in this case was quite enough to kill the man, and that the dose of tartar emetic was needless.'

John Conolly MD: '. . . that witness has never given a shower-bath of more than one minute flow; that witness would highly disapprove of a cold shower-bath of even ten minutes' duration, and would not order such a bath; that witness would not regard the administration of a shower-bath of 28 minutes' duration to any person, whether sane or insane, or under any circumstances of excitement, as medical treatment, and witness would not consider such a practice was either useful or justifiable; that in witness's opinion a cold-water shower-bath of 28 minutes' duration, followed by a dose of tartar emetic, would be so likely to be attended with fatal results, that witness would not take the responsibility of ordering it'.

Forbes Winslow, MD: '. . . that in witness's experience a patient in a maniacal state requires sustaining and not depletion; that although in such cases there is great excitement, with increased action of the heart and nervous system, it is an unnatural state, not resulting from constitutional power, and therefore should not be treated on the principle of lowering the patient; that the treatment used towards the patient, Dolley, was in every view of it unjustifiable, and, in witness's opinion, caused the man's death'.

21. *Lancet*, Vol.11, 12 July 1856.
22. *The Times*, 19 August 1856.
23. House of Commons Papers (1857) No. 77, 14, no. 77, Communications Respecting the Medical Superintendent of the Surrey Lunatic Asylum, (p. 28).
24. Ibid. (p. 40).
25. 'A letter to the Committee of the Surrey Lunatic Asylum, by Charles Snape, Medical

Superintendent (Male Department), in reference to the Case of Daniel Dolley (deceased)'; with an introduction, ibid. (p. 48).

26. For notes of the medical evidence given on this occasion, see House of Commons Papers (1857) No. 77, 14, no. 77, Communications Respecting the Medical Superintendent of the Surrey Lunatic Asylum (pp. 67–70), from which the following extracts are taken:

Dr Babington: '. . . I consider Mr Snape quite justified in what he has done; he had a right to suppose no injury would arise; he had tried long baths before on the same man with good effect, and as he was at this time more excited, a longer bath was reasonable, and a good effect might have been expected to result from it. The patient came out of the bath showing no ill effect; the cause of his death must be a matter of conjecture; he may have died from a fit; persons may die under chloroform even when administered for taking out a tooth, yet chloroform is used without objection. Shipwrecked sailors have often the cold sea dashing over them for hours, which yet does not injure them. In the case of this patient, there was only an extension of the treatment which, on former occasions, had been beneficial, and, under such circumstances, I should not have hesitated to act in the same manner as Mr Snape.'

Mr Bowman: 'I have read the whole of the evidence and Mr Snape's statement. I consider Mr Snape perfectly justified in his treatment of this patient, so far as I can judge, without personal experience of the management of lunatics or of the effect of shower-baths of long duration. Seeing that Mr Snape had found decided benefit from the uses of baths of 20 minutes' duration in many similar cases, as well as in this patient himself on former occasions, I think the extension to thirty minutes in this instance was reasonable, having regard to the fact that the attendant was directed to look at the man from time to time . . .'

Dr Todd: '. . . I think a man who had used long shower-baths with effect, as Mr Snape states he has done, would be quite justified in the treatment he has pursued in this case. I never used so long a bath. I would not use so long a bath without gradual experience. I cannot say the shower-bath killed the patient; he may have had some other disease not discovered, that occasioned his death. When a bath of 20 minutes' duration was known to be good, an extension to 30 minutes was a very natural course of practice, and might be thought a prudent and beneficial proceeding. When the duration of a shower-bath is extended from 20 to 30 minutes for the first time, it would be advisable that the medical officer should attend the administration of it personally . . .'

Dr Quain: '. . . I am not immediately conversant with the treatment of lunatics, but judging by Mr Snape's statement of his proceedings, and of his experience, which I take to be accurate, I do not consider that his treatment in this case was injudicious. The tartar emetic, in my opinion, had nothing to do with the death of the patient, which occured within two minutes after the dose had been administered. I cannot take upon me to say that Mr Snape was wrong in ordering the tartar emetic. I have had no experience of such a bath; but being assured that baths of 20 minutes' duration had been frequently found to be beneficial in persons of all ages, an extension of the bath to a duration of 30 minutes was not unreasonable . . .'

Mr Adison: '. . . Had I been asked my opinion respecting the treatment of the patient in question before I had read these papers, I should have had doubt; but having ascertained the effect of long baths as reported by Mr Snape, I consider he was justified in using the bath as he did, as a sedative – generally we use the bath as a stimulant. From the evidence, these long baths appear to have been very beneficial . . .'

27. Ibid. (pp. 41–8).
28. The Committee of Visiting Justices to Hanwell had seen fit to appoint a former army officer, with no previous experience of the treatment of the insane, above Conolly, as the 'Supreme Officer' at Hanwell. See R.A. Hunter & I. Macalpine, *Introduction* to reprint of John Conolly, *The Treatment of the Insane without Mechanical Restraints*, Dawsons, London, 1973.

3 The Physiognomy of Insanity (pp. 35-49)

1. 'The successful argument against mechanical restraint was, that although it kept the patient's body quiet, it really aggravated his malady: the question now which should be considered is, whether chemical restraint does permanent good, or whether by diminishing excitement at the ultimate cost of mental power it "makes a solitude and calls it peace" ' (Sir Henry Maudsley, *The Pathology of the Mind*, 1879; quoted in R.A. Hunter & I. Macalpine, *Three Hundred Years of Psychiatry, 1535–1860*, Oxford University Press, London, 1963 (p. 1033).
2. 'If the limitation of the direct therapeutical means applicable to mental disorders is so unsatisfactory, it is to be ascribed to the extreme obscurity in which the origin of cerebral disturbance is involved, and to the narrowness of our knowledge of the mental functions of the brain' (John Conolly, *The Treatment of the Insane without Mechanical Restraints*, 1856. Reprint: R. Hunter & I. Macalpine, Dawsons, London 1973, p. 76).
3. 'Although, in all probability, an exact knowledge of the nature of the nervous energy, and the causes of its irregularities, may never be attainable, there is reason to hope that the zeal with which mental physiology is now cultivated, and the careful observations to which the brain is subjected, will eventually throw more light on the structure and offices of many parts of the nervous system, and lead to results of great importance to medicine and to mankind. To confess our present ignorance is merely to acknowledge that our science is not yet brought to perfection; and to be scrupulous in interfering with functions of great importance, disturbed in a manner unintelligible to us, is only consistent with the rational and cautious character of modern medicine' (ibid., p. 77).
4. 'The physician's office is assuming, in these times, a higher character in proportion as he ceases to be a mere prescriber of medicines, and acts as the guardian or conservator of public and of private health; studious of all agencies that influence the body and the mind, and which, affecting individual comfort and longevity, act widely on societies of human beings . . . Obscurity may yet hang over the origin of mental derangement; the explanation of sudden recoveries may continue difficult; the alterations incidental to portions of nervous matter may baffle investigation, and the possible varieties in the condition of the blood, often apparently associated with mental disturbances, may yet be unknown, or incapable of satisfactory elucidation; but general means have been revealed to men of science conducing to important modifications and ameliorations of mental malady. Improved diet, lodging and clothing, greater personal cleanliness, and general sanitary regulations, have produced undeniably advantageous effects on the health and the duration of life of the insane' (ibid. (p. 79)).
5. See illustration 29. Sir Alexander Morison was also one of the most influential and tenacious opponents of the non-restraint system.
6. 'Another most important rule is to study the most extraordinary characters, examine the excess, the extreme of character, and the extreme of the opposite characters; at one time the most decisive traits of benevolent good, and at another of destructive evil; now the greatest of poets, next the dullest of prose writers; the idiot born and the man of genius. With this view visit hospitals for idiots. Begin with

drawing the grand outline of the most remark-able traits of the most stupid. Those first which all have in common; and next such as are individually peculiar. Having drawn what is particular, what is general will soon appear. From what is general, recur again to what is individual; describe and draw, draw and describe. Study each part; cover the other parts with the hands; consider the connection, the relation. Enquire where the decisive is to be found. Is it in this feature or in this? Select certain traits; and add them to the other features, that the combination and the effect of the whole may be found. Seek afterward for the company of men of wisdom and profound thought, and proceed as before' (J.C. Lavater, *Essays on Physiognomy Designed to Promote the Knowledge and Love of Mankind*, translated by Henry Hunter, London, 1789–92).

7. John Conolly, 'The Physiognomy of Insanity', No. 5: Mania and Convalescence, *Medical Times and Gazette*, 27 March 1858.

8. For a full account of Gall's work, see: Erwin H. Ackerknecht & Henry V. Vallois, *Franz Joseph Gall and His Collection*, Wisconsin Studies in Medical History, No. 1, University of Wisconsin Medical School, Wisconsin 1956.

9. 'Besides education, Gall was chiefly interested in reforms of the treatment of mental patients and of criminals. He submitted detailed plans for such reforms to different sovereigns, chiefly to the ruler of his native country, the Great Duchy of Baden. He himself planned to open a model hospital for mental patients in Vienna. His writings show a great knowledge of mental diseases and of the works of psychiatrists. His way of considering mental diseases as merely quantitative troubles of normal faculties and as diseases of the brain, contributed a great deal toward a better psychological and physiological understanding of patients who, much more so at that time than now, were the victims of moral condemnation' (ibid.).

10. John Conolly, 'The Physiognomy of Insanity', No. 7, Senile Dementia, *Medical Times and Gazette*, 15 May 1858.

11. Sir Charles Bell, *Essays on the Anatomy of Expression in Painting*, Longmans, London, 1806 (p. 155).
    On the subject of the *Outrageous Maniac* Bell wrote: 'The error into which a painter would naturally fall, is to represent this expression by the swelling features of passion and the frowning eyebrow; but this would only convey the idea of passion, not of madness. And the theory upon which we are to proceed in attempting to convey this peculiar expression of ferocity amidst the utter wreck of the intellect I conceive to be this, that the expression of mental energy should be avoided, and consequently all exertion of those muscles which are peculiarly indicative of sentiment. This I conceive indeed to be true to nature, but I am more certain that it is correct in the theory of painting. I conceive it to be consistent with nature, because I have observed (contrary to my expectation) that there was not that energy, that knitting of the brows, that indignant brooding and thoughtfulness in the face of madmen which is generally imagined to characterize their expression, and which we almost uniformly find given to them in painting. There is a vacancy in their laugh, and a want of meaning in their ferociousness.'

12. John Conolly, 'The Physiognomy of Insanity', No. 2: Suicidal Melancholy, *Medical Times and Gazette*, 16 January 1858.

13. Diamond sold this collection which later became part of the Hope Collection, now in the Ashmolean Museum, Oxford. The biographical material he put at the disposal of his friend J.C. Jeaffreson for his work *A Book about Doctors*, Hurst and Blackett, London 1861.

14. H.W. Diamond, 'On the Application of Photography to the Physiognomic and Mental Phenomena of Insanity', 1856.

15. Ibid.

16. 'The rage of the most savage animal is derived from hunger or fear. The violence of a madman arises from fear; and unless in the utmost violence of his rage, a mixture of fear will often be perceptible in his countenance. Often in lucid intervals, during the less confirmed state of the disease, they acknowledge their violence towards any particular person to have arisen from a suspicion and fear of their having intended some injury to them. This fact accounts for the collected shrunk posture in which a madman lies; the rolling watchful eye which follows you; and the effect of the stern regard of his keeper, which often quiets him in his utmost extravagance and greatest pertubation' (Sir Charles Bell, *Essays on the Anatomy of Expression in Painting*, Longmans, London 1806, p. 156).

17. John Conolly, 'The Physiognomy of Insanity', No. 3, General Melancholia, *Medical Times and Gazette*, 6 February 1858.

18. J.C. Bucknill, 'The Diagnosis of Insanity', *Asylum Journal of Mental Science*, Vol. 11, No. 18, 1856.

19. H.W. Diamond: 'On the Application of Photography to the Physiognomic and Mental Phenomena of Insanity', 1856.

20. In his report to the Committee of Visitors at Springfield for the year 1855, Diamond had already referred to the pleasure patients derived from prints hung in the wards: 'Your grant of a sum of money for the purchase of more books for the library, and also for prints

to adorn the walls of the wards, has been much appreciated by the patients; the books have been read constantly, and I have often noticed them standing contemplating the pictures, and they have expressed to me the pleasure they derive from them: and at the present not a single one has been injured.

'The liberality of Messrs Graves, Messrs Colnaghi and William Smith Esq, has enabled us to possess some engravings of a very superior character. We have at present about 300 prints; it is few however for the magnitude of the building, and I trust to be able to report to you further donations.'

21. John Conolly, 'The Physiognomy of Insanity', No. 9, Religious Mania, *Medical Times and Gazette*, 24 July 1858.

22. '*Application of Photography to Lunacy*. By T.N. Brushfield Esq, Superintendent of the County Lunatic Asylum, Chester. I have not had an opportunity of reading or knowing the contents of Dr Diamond's paper on photography as applied in the treatment, etc. of lunacy, beyond the ordinary newspaper article; but I have found, notwithstanding my imperfect attempts, that patients are very much gratified at seeing their own portraits, and more particularly when associated with a number of others on a large sheet of Bristol board, framed and hung up as an ordinary picture in the ward. In our worst female ward I have had a positive (on glass) framed and hung up for nearly eighteen months, and it has never yet been touched by any of the patients, although nearly all know whom it represents. Last week a patient, who was formerly óne of our most violent cases, begged for a portrait of herself, that she might send to her son, who was in Ireland, to show how much better she was.

'In the case of *criminal* lunatics, it is frequently of great importance that a portrait should be obtained, as many of them being originally of criminal disposition and education, if they do escape from the asylum, are doubly dangerous to the community at large, and they may frequently be traced by sending their photographs to the police authorities (into whose hands they are likely to fall), from some act of depredation they are likely to commit; the photographs would thus cause them to be identified, and secure their safe return to the asylum.

'With respect to those whose features cannot be made to assume a settled look, a highly sensitive collodion is necessary. I enclose a portrait of a patient whose expression of countenance varies every few seconds' (*Journal of the Photographic Society*, May 21, 1857).

Still, it should be noted that Conolly himself found something special in Diamond's work, as his frequent praises show. For example in the first of his articles on the physiognomy of insanity he wrote: 'Among those who now preside with so much advantage to the afflicted over the large asylums near London, no one, it is well known, has acquired a greater proficiency in this interesting art than Dr Diamond of the Surrey Asylum. His skill has, indeed, been exercised upon many of his friends, who are happily possessed of the intellectual faculties in high perfection, and some of these portraits have been shown in literary circles, and some contributed to the late exhibition in Manchester have excited very deserved admiration. This proficiency has also enabled Dr Diamond to enrich his portfolios with curious portraits of the insane, which are not only truthful as portraits, but revive in those familiar with insane patients the memory of many others whose various forms of mental peculiarity had made their characterisistic stamp; thus furnishing representations highly interesting, generally singular and striking, sometimes amusing, sometimes, it must be confessed, awful, but always suggestive of useful thought.'

23. R. Hunter & I. Macalpine, *Psychiatry for the Poor*, Dawsons, London, 1974 (p. 75).

24. John Conolly, *The Treatment of the Insane without Mechanical Restraints*, 1856. Reprint: R. Hunter & I. Macalpine, Dawsons, London, 1973 (p. 297).

25. As early as 1852 the following entry had appeared in *Notes & Queries* in an entry by W. Sparrow Simpson, BA, under the heading, 'Novel Applications of Photography': 'In the *Critic* for November 15, 1852 is the following statement, illustrative of the importance of photography, which may serve as a note of a new application of its powers: "The *Revue Génève* states that the Federal Council has authorized the department of justice and police to incur the charge of photographing the portraits of persons breaking the law by mendicancy in cantons where they have no settlement. It has found that the verbal descriptions hitherto relied on are insufficient to the identification of the offenders."

'What a curious picture gallery the police will ultimately form if this system is carried out!'

The Springfield Photographs
by Dr H.W. Diamond

1

Religious Melancholia (*see page 137*)

2

4

5

Insanity Supervening on Habits of Intemperance (*see page 151*)

6

General Melancholia (*see page 140*)

7

Senile Dementia (*see page 143*)

8

9

10

11

Suicidal Melancholy (*see page 138*)

12

Insanity Supervening on Habits of Intemperance (*see page 151*)

13

14

15

16

17
Chronic Mania (*see page 142*)

18

19

20

21

Melancholia Passing into Mania (*see page 141*)

The Bethlem Photographs
by Henry Hering

22

Religious Melancholia (*see page 149*)

23

Religious Melancholia Convalescence (*see page 149*)

24
Acute Melancholia

25

Convalescence after Acute Melancholia

26
Acute Mania

27
Convalescence after Acute Mania

28

Intermittent Mania

31

Intermittent Mania, Convalescent Stage

32

Apoplectic Mania. Infanticide

33
Epileptic Mania. Infanticide

38
Chronic Melancholia. Great Disposition to Suicide

40
Puerperal Mania

41

Convalescence after Puerperal Mania

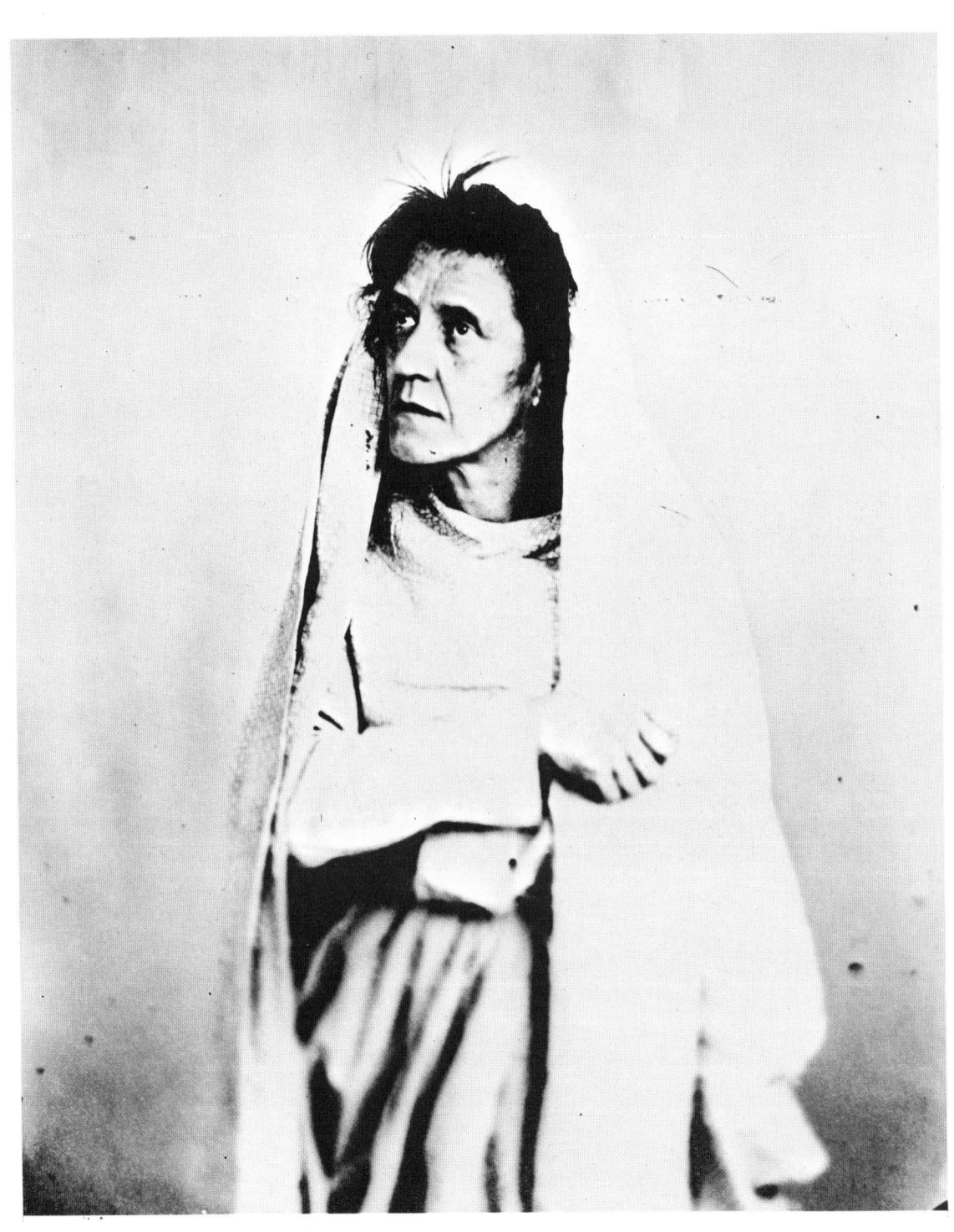

42

Intermittent Mania

43

Intermittent Mania. Convalescent Stage

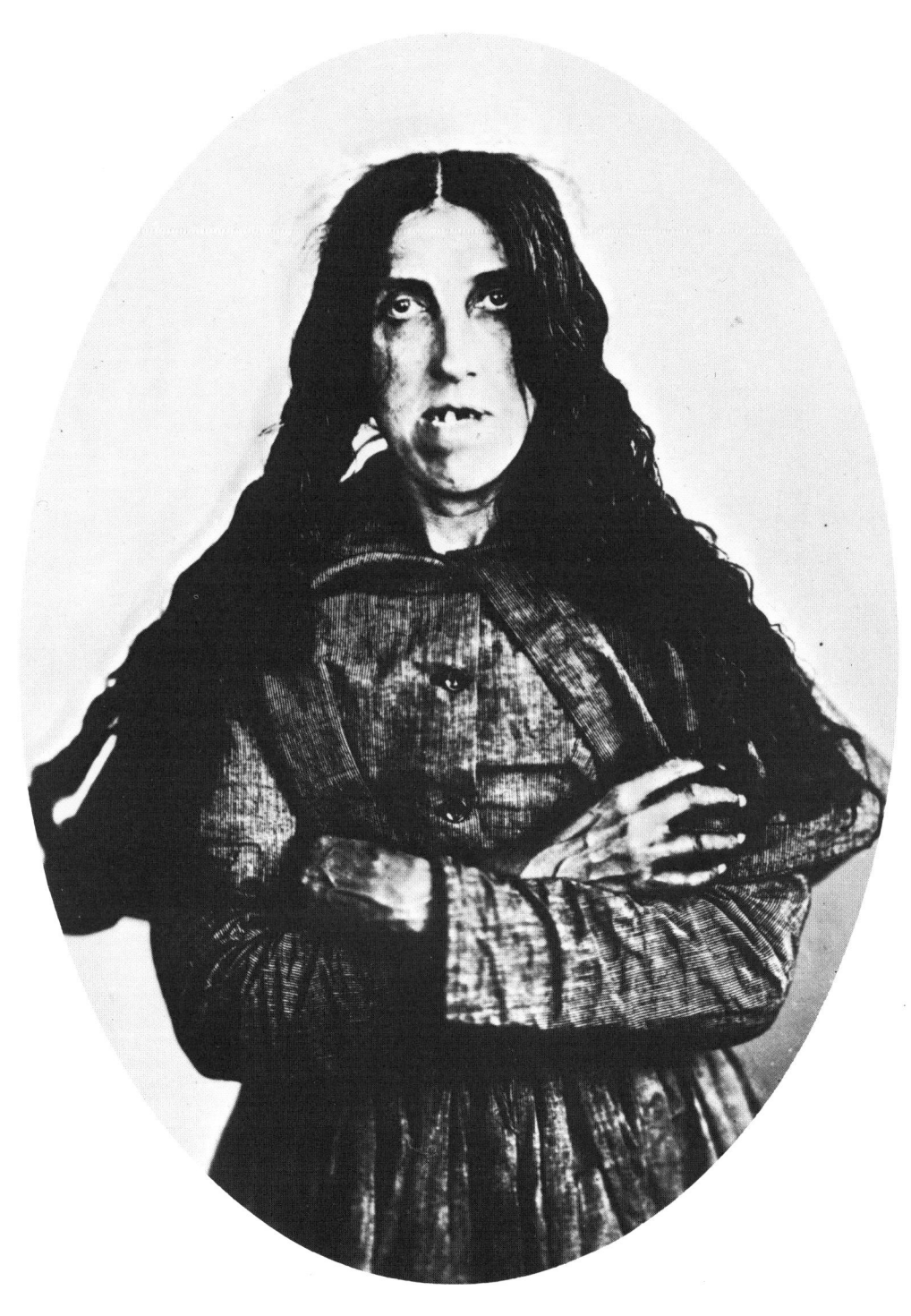

44
Acute Mania

45
Melancholia

46

Acute Mania (*see page 146*)

47
Convalescence after Acute Mania (*see page 148*)

48
Chronic Mania with Delusions

49

Melancholia

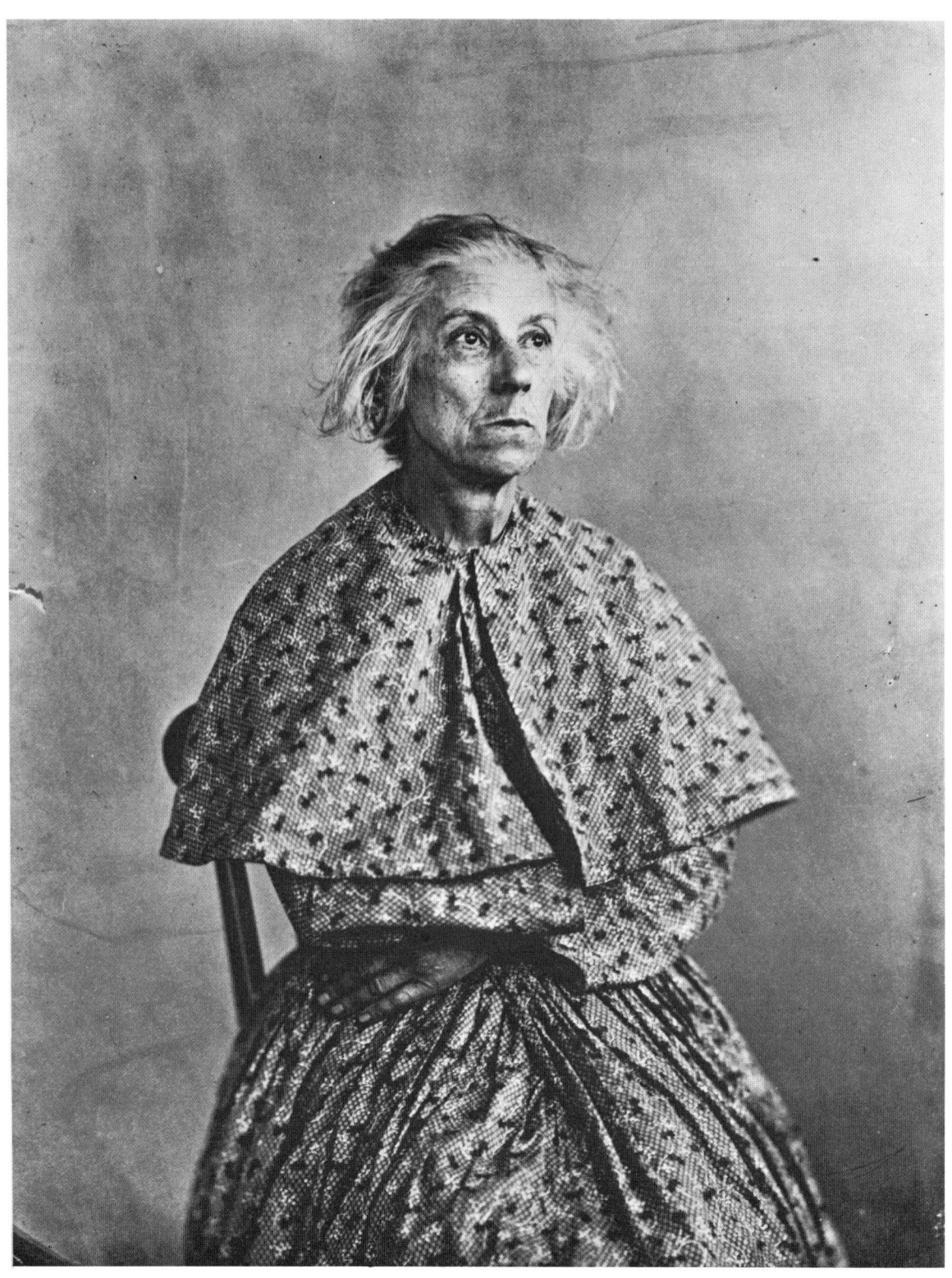

50

52
Acute Mania

53
Convalescence after Acute Mania

54

Chronic Dementia

55
Acute Dementia

56
Chronic Mania

57
Acute Melancholia. Father and Son

58
Mania Homicide

60
Ruffianism Homicide

61
Mania Homicide

63
Richard Dadd

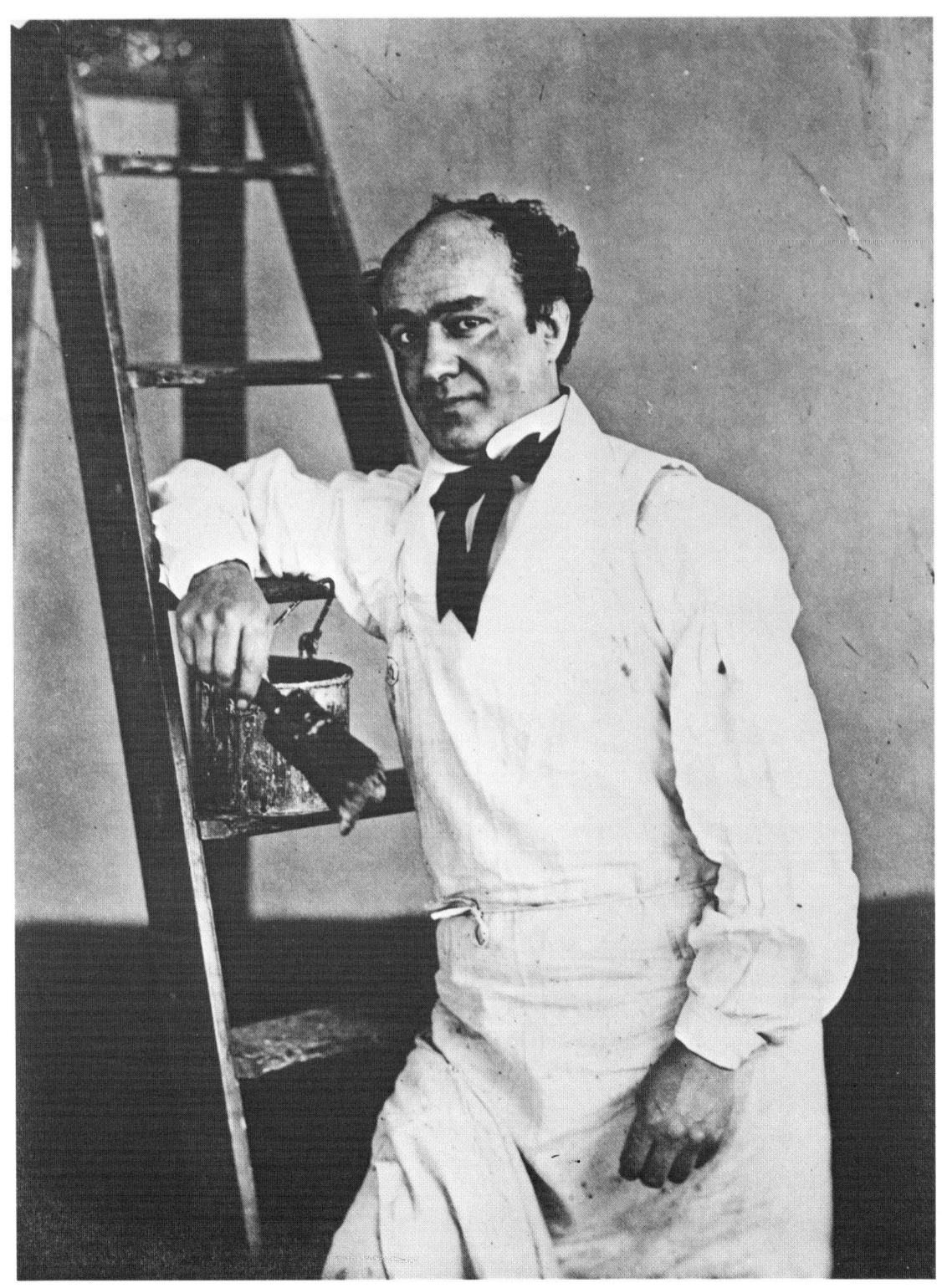

65
Mania Matricide

67
Ruffianism Homicide

68
Mania Homicide

70
Mania Homicide

71
Mania Matricide

Extracts from 'The Physiognomy of Insanity' by John Conolly

[Extracts from a series of thirteen articles published in the *Medical Times and Gazette*, January 1858 – February 1859]

No. 1 – Religious Melancholy

. . . In this form of melancholy there is no mere worldly despondency, nor thought of common calamities or vulgar ruin; but a deeper horror: a fixed belief, against which all arguments are powerless, and all consolation vain; a belief of having displeased the Great Creator, and of being hopelessly shut out from mercy and from heaven. . . . We discern the outward marks of a mind which, seemingly, after long wandering in the mazes of religious doubt, and struggling with spiritual niceties too perplexing for human solution, is now overshadowed by despair. The high and wide forehead, generally indicative of intelligence and imagination; the slightly bent head, leaning disconsolately on the hand; the absence from that collapsed cheek of every trace of gaiety; the mouth inexpressive of any varied emotion; the deep orbits and the long characteristic eyebrows; all seem painfully to indicate the present mood and general temperament of the patient. The black hair is heedlessly pressed back; the dress, though neat, has a conventual plainness; the sacred emblem worn round the neck is not worn for ornament. The lips are well-formed, and compressed; the angle of the jaw is rather large; the ear seems well-shaped; force of character appears to be thus indicated, as well as a capacity of energetic expression; whilst the womanly figure, the somewhat ample chest and pelvis (less expressed in the engraving

than in the photograph) belong to a general constitution out of which, in health and vigour, may have grown up some self-accusing thoughts in an innocent and devout, but passionate heart. For this perverting malady makes even the natural instincts appear sinful; and the sufferer forgets that God implanted them. . . . To escape future punishment, bodily mortifications must be endured: severe fasts, or some self-inflicted pain. Under these, the bodily strength, usually impaired in the commencement of the attack, becomes further impaired. The digestion becomes feeble, and even the sparest meals occasion suffering. Emaciation takes place; often proceeding to an extreme degree. The uterine functions (for the subjects of this form of malady are usually women), are suppressed. Paroxysms of excitement may occur, with sudden activity in the prosecution of schemes of vaguest import; but with these futile efforts misgivings become mingled. The thought of suicide, often suggested, becomes fixed; and such varied and ingenious efforts are made to carry it into effect as to demand incessant vigilance. . . .

. . . The subject of this photograph had left the Protestant faith, and become what is commonly called a Roman Catholic. Her education had not been such as to enable her to reason well on either side, and she became merely wavering and unsettled in her belief. Attention to ordinary matters was neglected; she sate [*sic*] in the attitude shown in the engraving for a long time together; she was negligent of her dress, and occasionally destructive of it. Often she cried out that she was a brute, and had no soul to be saved. . . .

It is unnecessary to say that her case was managed in the asylum with the most prudent caution. She was encouraged to more bodily exertion; and her mental perplexities, not being aggravated by reasonings unadapted to her, gradually died away. She soon began to occupy herself, and became useful in the laundry of the establishment. She was strengthened by quinine. The inactivity of the digestive canal, so common, or so constant in cases of melancholia, was counteracted by combining the *decoctum aloes compositum* with a tonic; and shower-baths, of half a minute's duration, contributed to restore general bodily energy. Such attacks never yield at once. They come on gradually, and depart slowly. After a residence of ten months in the asylum, this patient became well. It is gratifying to know that she remains well, having now left the institution seven months since.

No. 2 – Suicidal Melancholy

At first sight the portrait seems only that of a plain face, almost vulgar. Examined more closely, it becomes affecting. It speaks not of despondency merely, but of some horrible vision that has arisen in the mind. The hands are not only joined, as in ordinary examples of profound melancholy, but clasped, almost convulsively, finger within finger, with a muscular energy the expression of which the engraver has most ably

caught from the faithful photograph. By this wonderful art the muscles also of the right forearm are depicted as almost in immediate action; and the whole attitude of the patient shows the preponderating muscular strain existing on the same side of the body. The right shoulder is advanced; the right knee is drawn up

and pressed on the left. The inclination of the head to the right, the starting muscles on the left side of the neck, the excessive corrugation of the integuments of the forehead, all tell the same story of intense and painful emotion. All this energetic contraction seems to be produced by some fearful feeling. A further perusal of the face tells more than is revealed to a careless glance. The features are unrefined; but the wide and high head indicates intellectual qualities that cultivation might have improved; so as to control, perhaps, a now dominating ideality. The copious and dishevelled hair, which we feel sure must be black mingled with grey, is parted with no care, but straggles in sympathy with the tortured brain. Those many and curved wrinkles in the brow are not wrinkles of ordinary trouble.

The raised and equally curved eyebrows; the large, melancholy, and uplifted eyes, declare that the sense is fixed on some image of fear, which no other eye can detect; and the intensity of the prevalent emotion is forcibly expressed in all the other parts of the face. The upper eyelids disappear; the lower are strongly depressed; the muscles of the cheeks and the corners of the mouth are drawn down, the lower lip being, as it were, spasmodically acted upon, showing nearly all the front teeth of the lower jaw. The chin has been scratched and scarred by her own fingernails. The very ears seem starting forward. Everything bespeaks terror. You see that the suffering woman moves not; and that she holds little communion with those about her. Her whole aspect is intensely sorrowful, as well as full of alarm. She is, indeed, abstracted from the common world of sorrow and suffering, but lives in a world of dread alone.

. . . She was born of a mother on whom wretchedness had already done its work; and who was eccentric in mind, and eventually became paralysed. Her sole inheritance was poverty and labour, and a brain disposed to disease. In the portrait she looks old and worn, her real age being only 34. She was industrious, and led a correct life, and for a time managed to earn a living by straw-bonnet making. But this kind of labour is not very profitable, and, in order to ensure food and clothing, and the shelter of a roof, it was necessary for her to work fourteen hours a day. No pleasures, no healthful exercise, were part of her lot. Her mind was of an anxious cast; and she ever felt, no doubt, that the intermission of toil for a day or two would entail difficulty upon her, or the prospect of starvation. What other fears haunted the poor creature we cannot say; but after her mind had quite given way, her often-repeated expressions were, 'Oh! don't kill me, dear doctor!' 'Don't let anyone kill me!' At other times she would say, 'I am too wicked to live!' and then she would humbly say that she had not committed any wickedness; but had always been an industrious and good girl. The dread, however, of being murdered grew stronger and stronger. She still worked on, with no salutary variety of any kind, until, with the inconsistency of insanity, she began to think she might escape the danger by destroying her own life. She made many and desperate attempts to do this; attempts only frustrated by the watchfulness of those about her, and by the arrangements of a well-ordered asylum. She would conceal bits of window glass and try to cut her throat; or tear off a strip of sheeting, and throw it quickly over one of the gas-burners in the gallery in order to hang herself. But vigilance saved her again and again from the first danger, and she was preserved from the second by the slight fixing of the burners, made with a prospective regard to such possibilities.

No. 3 – General Melancholia

. . . Many a superintendent of an asylum, looking at this portrait, will be inclined to think he remembers such a man having been under his own care. I am myself very forcibly reminded by these photographic pictures of many cases familiar to me in the wards of Hanwell, in years gone by. Hopeless and worn-out men, and desponding and terrified women, constituted a considerable proportion of the cases admitted from distant workhouses or from homes of destitution. In many instances such a state was but a painful ending of a life of joyless struggle. The female patients, in whom melancholia had often supervened on bodily illness, recovered in time, in larger proportion than the men. The women were usually more imaginative, and their fears were more various. In the men, depression seemed to have grown gradually out of realities; out of the hopelessness of over-coming the perpetual enemy with which they had honestly contended almost from boyhood to middle age; and, when once overcome, they rallied no more. The enemy was poverty.

The subject of the Illustration accompanying the present paper is one presenting the kind of solemn hopelessness arising out of long and unavailing efforts to keep just above poverty; and out of the diminution of nervous energy which becomes generally perceptible in the working man at this time of life. Probably both circumstances conjoined have brought him to this. He is sixty years old, and has all his life been a working gardener; sober in his habits, conduct-ing himself well in the affairs of life, and

139

expression and attitude; the drooping head, the sight unemployed on surrounding objects, the hands resting on the thighs, and the mental revelations of the eyelids, and of the forehead, and of the protruded underlip; with the line drawn from the angle of the nose to the mouth, as well that line of age and care drawing down the corner of the mouth itself: all convey to the student of the human face, that, with failing nutrition hope has failed also; that the patient has come to a conclusion that insuperable trouble has fallen upon him, and that, ever meditating upon this, still he finds no way to escape.

Dulness [*sic*], therefore, the advancing shadow of the dulness of death, rests upon him, never in this world to be withdrawn.

No. 4 – Melancholia Passing on to Mania

. . . In the engraving accompanying the fourth of these papers, the singular combination of muscular actions attending the mixed state of a patient's mind when one form of mental disorder is passing into another, as melancholia into mania, seems to be curiously expressed. The corrugation of the frontal muscles is seen to have given way to transverse wrinkles, and a partial elevation of the eyebrows, the eye having at the same time assumed an active character; as if the patient was now beginning to understand some plot, and to discern some enemies, of which the belief had obscurely oppressed her in her melancholy state; and distinct ideas of revenge were beginning to excite her. . . .

Her story is but one in a large chapter of such which London furnishes. She gained a small livelihood by the occupation of a sorter and folder of paper, and lived but poorly. After a confinement she had an attack of puerperal mania, lasting about six months; her conversation was generally incoherent, and her actions were sometimes impulsive and violent. She repudiated her infant, declaring that it did not belong to her, and on one occasion she leaped out of a window fourteen feet from the ground. About a month after being received into the Surrey Asylum the excitement left her, and great despondency supervened. She then sate all day in one position, or else stood up covering

reported to be of pleasant manners. But, although his occupation was one which a great authority declares to be the purest of human pleasures, and the greatest refreshment to the spirits of man, it could not ward off the invasion of slowly and obscurely working causes of decay. His power of being industrious died away; his pleasant manners left him; and some months since he fell unaccountably into a state of apathy or of vague despondency; his silence only broken by moaning and lamentation; and yet retaining a capability of making a rational reply to words directly addressed to him. The good form of the head; the shape, especially, of the anterior and upper head, and the submissive expression of the features, where we find no trace of violent passions or of evil habits, are distinctly marked. We read the clear impress in the whole face of an honest man. But the eye is sunken into the socket; the grey hair hangs straight, as is usual in age; and, although he is not very far advanced in years, the withered frame and settled hopeless look, and the general

emotion, and the eyebrows, although corrugated, have not the tense contraction toward the nose, which is observable in many cases of melancholia. The lips are not drawn down at the angles, but, although well shaped, are somewhat compressed, and the lower jaw indicates some half-formed determination. The maniacal condition of this patient has been accompanied with such an increase of stoutness that subsequent photographs are scarcely to be recognized as being likenesses of the same patient.

No. 6 – Chronic Mania and Melancholy

. . . Comical as this picture of an old woman appears at the first view, it tells a somewhat lamentable tale of long mental vexation . . . The apparently careless air, the reversed bonnet, and a sort of drollery lurking in the cheeks and chin, are largely mixed with traces both of former agitation and excitement, and also with some shadows of lost hope and joy. Activity, and a certain strength of character seem depicted in the general form of the face; in the well-formed forehead, wide and high; in the broad and pronounced chin; in the development of the superciliary region of the brow, and, perhaps, even in the nose. One feels sure that once this poor woman was of a merry mind, and danced and sung, and turned her bonnet round for very mirth. Even now there is something in the position of her head and her general attitude which betokens a consciousness of being an odd and amusing object presented to the casual visitor; but the delvings of care in the forehead and in the whole face are still many and deep: the strong descending lines from the *alae nasi* to the depressed corners of the mouth, speak of alternations of depression with excitement, and make the physiognomy indicative of past attacks of mania and melancholia, both of which have left their traces there.

This odd facial expression, and the combination of various expressions, seem, indeed, to be the natural results of what was known to have been her mode of life. She was by occupation a washerwoman, and, no doubt, for a time active and hard-working. Advancing to middle age, and beginning to feel the exhaustion incidental to daily labour, she began to seek the resource of

her face with her hands. She never employed herself, and would not reply when spoken to. For many months she remained in this state, and then what at first appeared to be recovery took place, and her faculties seemed to revive. The melancholia, however, soon returned, and continued six months more. Then, a sudden renewal of bodily and mental energy occurred, and she became maniacal; began to dress herself fantastically, sung songs, and indulged in various ideas connected with wealth and pleasure, in which state she at present remains. The photograph, taken when the state of melancholy was passing into that of excitement, retains something of the fixedness of attitude and expression in the first state; as in the arms held close to the body, and the position of the lower extremities, and in the downward tension of the cheek. The body is thin, and the hair is lank and heavy. But the eyes are not lost in vacancy; they seem to discern some person or object which excites displeasure or suspicion. The forehead is wrinkled with some strong temporary stimulants, and, soothed and stupefied with gin, became less and less careful as to food, or to food of a good description: for gin seems to silence hunger as it silences conscience. She became occasionally violent, and at length unmanageable except in an asylum; to which she was taken seventeen years ago. The regular life led there, the good food, the general regulations of the place, and occasional medical treatment, had their usual good effects. In the laundries of our large asylums near London such cases abound. You see a number of active women, busy at the washing-tub, or dexterous in mangling and folding, but whose air and manner, and somewhat fiery countenance, show that they are not always so composed; and, indeed, the nerves of visitors are generally more

likely to be shaken in the crowd of these useful but eccentric laundresses than elsewhere; for it is the custom of many of them, on some sudden impulse, to break off from work at once, and exhibit much violence of voice and gesture. Formerly the nurses, as excited as the patients, used to overpower them and carry them off by main force to the refractory ward, in their progress to which their shouts and remonstrances diffused alarm over nearly the whole building. They are now understood much better. The peculiar form and duration of such outbreaks in these hard-working women are quite familiar to the head-laundress and her assistants; and by observing a rule of very wide application and utility in managing asylums – the rule of letting them alone – the most obstreperous among them, after satisfying her mind by the unrestrained expression of her uncontrollable anger, will resume all the activity of the washerwoman, and perhaps give no more trouble for weeks to come.

Such appears to have been the character of the old lady in the reversed bonnet. But the maniacal attack being the first she had experienced, and occurring when at a curable age – a little more than forty – the asylum influences had a happy effect upon her, and in about eleven months she was discharged cured. But there are patients who seem, however apparently well, still to require this external influence to keep their minds rational; and this poor woman appears to have been one of them; for although it was said that she did not relapse into intemperate habits as to drinking, she was not found to be an endurable neighbour when at large, and was very soon taken back to the asylum.

If favourably situated, patients of this description commonly become calmer with advancing years. Occasional tricks, and fits of passion, now and then occur; but they give little trouble. Age is already telling on this subject of chronic mania. The countenance, although not wholly sad, has nothing comfortable in it. The aged head, inclined to one side; the drooping of the right shoulder; the listless and pendent arms; seem to indicate the weariness of one long driven about by various disturbing passions, and whose grey hairs will soon lie in the grave in which, at length, rest comes to the troubled, and peace to the turbulent.

No. 7 – Senile Dementia

The Illustration accompanying the present paper represents the last stage of mental life in a man of great acquirements and well-exercised mind. In such men, if they are also blessed with a tranquil temperament, the approaches of age are gradual, and scarcely painful; or, at least, the gradual failure of bodily strength, the less vigorous digestion, the diminished desire for voluntary muscular exertion, are borne patiently. Quiet pleasures remain: a love of reading; an interest in other men's activity; a sympathy with the vigorous exertions of younger relatives, and with their achievements, if they achieve anything; and also a fondness for the progress of scientific or moral truth. It is not until the individual begins to recognize that his mental powers are also obeying the universal law, and losing their activity or their power, that he begins to feel the sorrow that is incurable, or

which will only yield to insensibility. . . . In this Illustration we fancy that we see represented an individual on whom the oblivion of years has crept gently: one who has gone on day after day, for a great part of his life, with occupations demanding talent and accuracy, but of which he was perfectly master. By slow degrees he grew incapable of continuous attention to minutiae, now and then became puzzled, now and then forgetful, and dreamy and drowsy; wondering, meanwhile, what soporific influence was overshadowing him, and comparing himself to a man in a kind of mesmerized sleep. The figure represents a venerable ruin. In the finely developed head we seem to read an equally well-balanced mind; without extravagance, without extremes. The eye is large and meditative, the nose well pronounced, the lower jaw indicative of steadiness and strength. In the upper lip there is, perhaps, a want of compression, belonging to the approaching dementia. The whole figure, and also the drooping eyelid, bespeak repose. It is happy for old men when this repose is seldom disturbed. Few of them are so privileged as not to feel from time to time a sort of pang of mental dissolution, or something like sensible accessions of old age, and an unavailing sorrow that all they valued perishes in this world, even as the less regarded elements of their bodies. And to mortal man such mortal experiences are real afflictions. To find the sight less acute, and the ear blunted and treacherous, and the limbs heavy, and the voice tremulous; and, worse than all, the glorious faculties of the mind gathering some strange dimness, the reflection faulty, and the imagination fickle and flighty, is to be sensible of the approaches of death; and actually to feel how gradually and yet how surely 'this sensible warm motion' is becoming 'a kneaded clod'.

No. 8 – Puerperal Mania

. . . In the *first* of the four portraits of a case of this kind, there is represented a short initial stage of dulness and apathy. The patient was very quiet, and even sullen when addressed: she remained nearly all day in one posture, her hands crossed and resting on her knees, after the manner of melancholic patients; but the countenance, it will be seen, rather expresses bewilderment than unmixed depression; the eyes are directed forward; there is no very marked drawing down of the corner of the mouth or of the chin, and there is a slight elevation of the upper part of the cheeks; altogether, rather indicative of some advancing reverie, more agreeable than talk, or even than food; and this patient was indeed not only sullen when spoken to, but refused food, partly, perhaps, because she feared to abandon the reverie.

There was, however, a depression mingled with her reveries, arising, as it would appear, from real circumstances. She had been an industrious woman, of good character; but she and her husband were poor, and, contemplating, probably, the difficulty of providing food, clothes and shelter for a coming family, her husband left her and his home and his country to seek employment in Australia. The sensitive wife, whose mother had been insane, became deranged and melancholic, almost as soon as her poor little child came into the world of want, in which the father was so perplexed how to provide against starvation. But in a few days the memory of real events died away, and the malady assumed the form most generally seen after delivery. All the harassing troubles of life were forgotten, and husband and baby and her lonely home. The *second* portrait was taken eight days after the first. Her features were then not only lively, but mirthful; the mouth is drawn out laterally, the nostrils are expanded, and the lively eyes, the elevated eyebrows, and the merry cheeks and chin are felicitously rendered in the plate. She still sits with her hands crossed, and resting on her knee; but she looks as if she might easily be persuaded to get up and dance. She was, indeed, generally singing; she tore her clothes out of an excess of animal spirits; and she now took food, not only willingly but voraciously.

In about six weeks from the commencement of the malady, a great change took place, and recovery seemed to commence. She became quite comfortable, and was employed in needlework; but had a somewhat impatient desire to go away from the asylum. At this time the *third* portrait was taken. She is seen standing up, and neatly dressed. Her face has lost its broad merriment; but there is a tension of the facial muscles, which prevents the experienced Physician from concluding that all the malady has yet passed away. Perfect muscular composure has not yet been established. In accordance with these prognostics, in a fortnight afterward she relapsed into the state of drollery and destructiveness portrayed in the second portrait. Happily, the relapse was only temporary, and in ten days more she was again industrious, and quite tranquil. From this time she remained so; and when her recovery was confirmed by a month or two more of observation, which the relapse had made advisable, she left the asylum quite well – an event commemorated by the *fourth* portrait; wherein she is represented in bonnet and shawl, with composed features and pleasant honest face, animated still, but no longer excited; her general appearance indicating the restoration of the health and the strength to be sufficiently called upon in the undertaking now meditated, of taking out her baby and rejoining her poor husband in Australia.

These four portraits were, I believe, the first attempts of Dr Diamond to delineate, by photography, the progressive changes in the countenance in mental disease.

144

PUERPERAL MANIA IN FOUR STAGES.

From a Photograph by Dr Diamond.

No. 9 – Religious Mania

. . . The subject of this portrait was the wife of a labouring man – not of the wretched class of labourers familiar to us round about London, whose habitations, dress, manners, habits and half-naked and rude children, disfigure the waysides of the beautiful environs of the metropolis; but of the labouring class of a province two hundred miles further north in our island, where decent cottages, often picturesque, and always scrupulously clean, are inhabited by hard-working men, attached to the neighbouring farmers and landowners, and to the soil; and who contrive by honest labour to procure wholesome food, good clothing, or clothing kept in careful repair; and have decent beds to lie upon: and who, when God's day returns, a day sacred from muscular toil and worldly care, may also be seen gathered together in humble but decent raiment, in those quiet and beautiful old village churches on which the railway traveller has but time to indulge a passing glance. . . .

There is, however, no retreat so rustic, no spot so secure, as to be wholly protected from perturbations of the senses, and of the heart, and of the conscience, and of the mind. Even the religion derived from indisputable authority seems too simple, too pure, and too serene for the faculties of human beings to receive and cherish and profit by, unless recommended either by pomps and gauds and vanities on the one hand, or by vain imaginations and nervous excitement on the other. Thus in small villages and in rural churches, the ordinary ritual appearing too dull and too scantily inspiriting, enthusiastic singing, earnest prayers recommended by strenuous physical action, and long sermons, in which the free reins are given to the excited fancy, supply the stimuli apparently welcome in the most secluded districts; and the sounds issuing from humble chapels fill the summer air of evening, and attract the common people with a force quite irresistible.

. . . Among the gratifications soon deemed necessary, or at least permitted, were prayer-meetings, where each enthusiast prayed and confessed in his or her own wild way; and also what are called love-feasts, meetings where the

feelings are even more highly excited by the prayers, by the sweet congregational singing of affecting or of joyous hymns, and by the condensed enthusiasm incidental to such an assembly of fervent human beings, who unconsciously, and almost inevitably, must permit human affections to mingle with divine in such tumult of the soul.

It was at one of these meetings that the subject of the portrait, whose history led to the mention

of them, laid the foundations of unreason. . . . The patient . . . was an excellent wife, remarkable for industry, for the respectability of her character, and leading a domestic life, free not only from vice but from irregularity; and she was earnestly devout. She was induced, with no great difficulty, to partake of the attractive pleasures of the love-feast, an exceptional variety in the dull and uneventful existence of the village in which she dwelt. The temporary consequences were lamentable. She became much excited during the festival; and for a time the excitement did not subside. The control of the mind was gone; and, although a kind of calm followed on returning to quiet, daily duties, it was not the calm of peaceful promise;

but the prelude to stormy disturbance of the feelings and passions, and the wild exercise of all the frantic words and deeds which are among the transformations of mania, and to which no experience can render the observer insensible. . . .

. . . Even when this portrait was taken, some slight return to calmness had begun to be perceptible, so that she could be persuaded to sit still for a short period. But generally she was noisy, quarrelsome, ever on the alert to produce discomfort and disturbance among those by whom she was surrounded. She was destructive of things about her, tearing her own clothing, and breaking all the fragile furniture of the ward; her habits became not negligent only, but dirty; her hands were employed in mischief, and her tongue was the constant instrument of calumny. Her language was coarse, often indelicate, sometimes blasphemous. Her very appearance became so repulsive that the other patients avoided her. This pitiable state continued for many weeks; her almost perpetual excitement appeared to defy sleep and rest, and her fierce excitement and vociferous denunciations of those near her, knew little or no intermission by night or by day. . . .

After being several weeks at Bethlehem [sic], it became practicable to take her portrait; and she was very willing to have it done. . . . One incidental effect of these artistical amusements is to draw the attention of the patients themselves to their own costume, and sometimes also to their general appearance, as to face and figure; and this direction of their notice may lead to salutary results. In the case in question, the patient made some objection to her own dress, which she evidently thought not very becoming; and she at length made it a condition of her sitting quiet that she should be represented with a book in her hand. The book, indeed, was held upside down; but it did quite as well. Her sense of propriety was gratified, and her face shows that she required no printed page to suggest thoughts to her yet busy mind. . . .

Those accustomed to the observation of faces will recognize . . . the wide, high, and thoughtful brow; and the observers of heads will as readily discern, in the lateral regions, the characteristic arch resulting from the full development of the localities marked by phrenologists as the seats of marvellousness and ideality; whilst from the forehead to the crown of the head, or as far as the band of hair permits our tracing them, the forms associated with veneration and firmness are equally legible, with a suspicion of ascending to too exalted a height. . . .

. . . The eyes are fixed on the book beneath them, as on a Bible from which texts rise before them; the depression of the inner angle of the eyebrows still more forcibly marks this, and also the compression of the upper lip, and the slight uplifting of the outer angles of the lower: but still the eyebrows are raised, and there are traces of expression, but which words cannot distinctly express, in the upper portion of the cheeks, beneath the eyes, which convey the sense of the mind being moved by some new and delightful conviction. Roundness of chin and strength of the lower jaw, without angularity, seem to bespeak the earnestness of her character; and are also, it may be presumed, allied with the fervour or the energy usually present with a full developed cerebellum. The eyeballs are directed to the right-hand page of the large book, and all her expression and attitude tends to that direction, as in a reader too wholly interested to move the book; and the heavy book itself is upheld by hands untired by the exertion, yet not at liberty to smooth down the leaf that floats between the upside-down pages and the enthusiast's eyes.

. . . But no adequate idea can be formed of the modification of natural expression wrought even in this patient by mental perturbation, until this present portrait is presented in contrast with the recovered face, which will form the subject of the next illustration.

No. 10 – Religious Mania – Convalescence

. . . There is no dulness or rustic stupidity to be seen in her face. The forehead is unusually good, and the whole head may, without exaggeration, be called beautiful. The observing and the intellectual regions of the forehead are in admirable proportion to each other; and the region of veneration is so grandly marked as to rejoice any phrenologist; while its combination with the ample ideality and marvellousness

147

seems to explain the peculiar form in which her mental disturbance manifested itself. The fixed and almost intense expression of the eyes, and the recovery, as it were, of her eyebrows from the undue elevation of mental excitement, are worthy of regard. Even the nose belongs to an intelligent face; and the shape of the lips is indicative of delicate perception. The fine

contour of the chin, and the firm character of the lower part of the face, are sufficiently observable; but, as an illustration of what has been said of the difficulty of describing modifications of facial muscular action, there is a gentle smile pervading the features, to which it would be in vain to attempt to assign any narrow locality. Whoever is interested in remarks of this kind, and feels more than mere curiosity concerning the workings of malady on the nerves of facial expression, and on those which conduce by their action to expression in attitude, will doubtless dwell more minutely on these two portraits, comparing them with the attention they deserve. The loose and negligent dress in the first portrait, the neglected state of

the hair, the general impression of a preoccupied imagination in the face, and especially in the lips and eyebrows, may be curiously compared with the carefully arranged costume, indicative of neatness and taste, and with the resuscitated mind shining through all the features in the second. It is evident that the patient must, in her sound state, be even superior to the generality of women of her station, and one whom a liberal education might have preserved from the influence of vulgar fanaticism. Too true, indeed, it is, that at the present time a very large proportion of what are called educated women are found among those affected with religious insanity.

No. 11 – Religious Melancholia

. . . Conditions of the brain and the nerves of which we possess no accurate knowledge, sometimes inherited, sometimes following too much excitement, mental or bodily, sometimes apparently associated with morbid conditions of the stomach and liver, and in very many cases with uterine disorder, modify all impressions made on the senses and affections in such a way as to render them all sources of pain, or at least of discomfort. Patients who present this peculiarity have certainly for the most part the external signs of melancholic temperament; a dusky and partially flushed complexion, tinged now and then with yellow; the head well formed anteriorly; the forehead broad, but usually deficient in height; the vertex often high, and the occipital region broad and bulging; the expression of the face gloomy, and strongly contrasted with the occasional smiles evoked from time to time by cheerful friends, as if without the will of the despairing patients themselves. Over-exertion of the mind brings on this melancholy state in men of great mental power, and leads often to a wish for death, and to meditations for effecting it. By perfect mental rest they recover. The same over-tasking of the brain, although more by domestic responsibilities than intellectual exertions, leads, in women of high conscientious feelings, to the same depression. In all these cases the tendency to self-destruction is commonly observable.

. . . Unfortunately, the temperament which

seems most open to impressions of pain and discouragement when exposed to the common chances and occupations of life was in this case exemplified by previous attacks, on three occasions, although the patient was but twenty-three years of age. Great mental anxiety, incidental to a responsible charge undertaken by her, had been the apparent cause of each attack. In each attack, loss of appetite, and a great sadness of countenance were the precursory symptoms observed by her friends. Entire refusal of food was the next step; and by day and night the afflicted woman wandered up and down her room, moaning and lamenting her lot. The restlessness for a time went on increasing, and a disposition to injure herself arose, requiring much protective vigilance from those about her. When it became necessary to remove her to the asylum her face was disfigured by self-inflicted scratches and scars, not represented in the engraving. The eyebrows are seen drawn into puckers expressive of inward suffering; and the upper eyelids droop over the downcast eyes. Beneath the lower eyelids there are furrows, seemingly the furrows of tears: and images of sorrow surely exist within the dreamy gloom of that preoccupied vision. There is a

sorrow expressed, not of sinful memories, but of fatal cares that cannot be resisted. The patient is still young; the angles of the mouth are not yet drawn rigidly down, as commonly seen in older cases, but there are depressions near them which foretell what will be, and there are very deep lines descending from above the *alæ* of the nose, premature lines of a later physiognomy. The lower lip is depressed by the prevalent sorrowful thoughts; and the body and head droop in opposite directions. But there is a great, and perhaps unavoidable, omission in this engraving, which could scarcely be in the original photograph; for it is surely meant in the first of the two portraits to show that the patient was sitting down, and those amputated forearms should have ended in clenched hands. . . . Upon the whole, there is in this portrait an expression of intense distress, concentrated, inward, reflecting, but with no tendency to violent demonstration. . . .

Yet, although there is a quiet misery only expressed in the first of these two portraits, there is a very appreciable difference between the first portrait and the second. Whether the seasons influence the mind is a question which, though long since settled by the vulgar, is considered by some philosophers as one which merely encourages the fumes of a vain imagination. In this case, however, the cold and variable season of spring passed away and no change took place in the patient's doleful mind; and when June came with its genial sunshine, her watchful and kind physician perceived a return of brightness and activity in his poor patient. Her melancholy thoughts, fixed only on self, disappeared; her mild and amiable character again shone forth; she gratefully acknowledged that her own heart was freed from the pressure of care, and it became her pleasure to console others whose bosoms were still clogged with perilous stuff, and to comfort those still labouring under sadness. . . .

The second portrait, taken during this happy convalescence, was doubtless taken while the patient was standing up; which would have been better shown if anything in the first had made the sitting posture manifest. As it is, the patient seems to have grown taller, and the altered position of the head makes the forehead seem higher. The happier mental state is still well shown in the general composure of the face; and, although the meditative and conscientious character is quite readable, the acute distress is evidently gone: the eyebrows have lost their wavy or puckered character, and are gently arched, without excess: the eyes, clear and well opened, the diminished depth of the diverging lines from above the *alæ nasi*, and the calm character of the well-formed lips, are all distinguishable. In the figure there is no longer the drooping of despondency; and in the dress there are marks of greater care than was consistent with the hopeless state now recovered from.

A consideration of the temperament of this patient, and of the previous attacks, cannot but create an apprehension of returns of her unhappy malady; and although in such recurrent affliction patients will return voluntarily to the asylums where they experienced kindness, and where they recovered, there is something dreadful in the prospect of such relapses; and their prevention in every such case should occupy the most serious attention, if any opportunity is given to a Medical Practitioner of seeing the patient occasionally. . . .

No. 12 – Insanity Supervening on Habits of Intemperance

The portraits accompanying this paper are illustrative of some of the modifications of features and expression in women who have fallen into the habits of intemperance, on which derangement of the mental powers has ensued to a greater or less extent. The two portraits represent different patients, of different character and of different history. The poor creature on the right having been nurtured in low life, almost brought up in early acquired habits of drinking, left to do their sure and uninterrupted work on body and mind until both have acquired the impress of a misfortune unavoidable, and slowly ripened into vice, and bringing the whole creature into a sort of chronic and indelible appearance of sottishness. In the left-hand portrait is represented another patient, of a respectable station in life, but also ruined by drink. . . .

Although we perceive even in this portrait the somewhat bloated or swollen condition of the fleshy parts of the face which tipsy habits produce, much expression remains – but it is of wretchedness and despair. The raised hands, pressed together, indicate the intensity of her prominent emotions; the eyes, somewhat uplifted, but gazing on nothing; the deep corrugation of the overhanging integuments of the lower forehead, portray the painful questioning of a woman not forgetful of her former life, nor unconscious of the comfortless change that has come over her; and the expression is heightened by those undefinable modifications of the muscular structure of the cheeks which add so much to all facial expression of intense character. In the upraised under lip, also, and in the tensely elevated chin, there is so much meaning of the same kind, that we might almost fancy the poor patient breaking out, in this suffering mood, into expressive words, as was indeed the poor women's custom. . . : Her history was indeed lamentable. She had been well educated, and resided, when a young woman, with her mother, who possessed a little independent property. Being then good-looking, she was much noticed; nor did it appear that she

lost her station by any immorality of early life. But she was not watched enough to guard her from pernicious acquaintances, who enjoyed, it would seem, the perverse satisfaction of teaching her the poor pleasures arising from the taste of spiritous liquors, until she adopted Mrs Gamp's plan of putting gin into the teapot. Somehow, as always happens in such cases, the little property possessed by her mother gradually diminished, and at length disappeared altogether. Dram-drinking became the only remaining comfort of the impoverished house; and thus things went on until one article of furniture after another, and also the clothes of her mother and herself, passed into the hands of the pawnbrokers. The poor mother found shelter in the workhouse, and the still more unhappy daughter, torn by remorse, and maddened more and more by intemperance now grown habitual, became maniacal, and was received into the lunatic asylum. Much of this, perhaps all of it, is written in that despairing, questioning face. Memory of the past and purer time has not been destroyed by her malady, nor conscience obliterated. She feels herself transformed, and that for her no earthly joy remains or will return. Her irritable hands have traced marks of agony on her forehead; her neglected curls hang raggedly

over her ears; she has torn them away until she is nearly bald. Even her large and well-developed brain seems to impress the beholder with thoughts aggravative of the miserable desolation that now alone prevails in the depths of her consciousness and memory. There is no healthful action and no comfort in any corner of that restless brain. Where once there was quick perception, imagination, benevolence, under-standing, there is now but a tumultuous succession of ineffaceable records, read by the light of madness only, with no ray of better light from the retrospection, and as yet no higher hope. Suicide, the last resource of such wretched-ness, has been often attempted by her. . . .

A different history from the preceding is plainly enough written in the right-hand portrait . . . Here the bloated face, the pendulous masses of cheek, the large lips uncontrolled by any voluntary expression, and to which refine-ment and delicacy seem never to have belonged; the heavily gazing eyes, not speculative, scarcely conscious; the disordered, uncombed, capri-ciously cut hair, cut with ancient scissors or chopped with impatient knife; the indolent position of the body, and the heavy resting of the coarse, unemployed, outstretched fingers, together with the neglected dress and reckless

151

abandon of the patient, all concur to declare the woman of low and degraded life, into whose mind, even before madness supervened, no thoughts except gross thoughts were wont to enter; and whose bold eye and prominent mouth were never, even from early infancy, employed to express any of the higher or softer sensibilities of a woman's soul. But yet she is, even in this degraded state, more truly an object of pity than of condemnation. It is easy to condemn – is harder to be just. Where this now outcast human being was born, and how brought up, it were vain to inquire. She probably never had a home; and it appears, in fact, that her earliest reminiscences were only of gaining a kind of livelihood by selling miscellaneous articles in the streets; articles begged, or articles lent, or articles stolen, no doubt. As she grew up, gross appetites grew up also; the love of beer, among the rest, developed itself strongly; and she was well-known to her familiars as what even they denominated a low-lived person. But beer was sometimes hard to procure; it could not always be successfully begged for; it could not be easily stolen; and it could not be bought without money. So the want of this stimulant joy of low life caused her to cultivate her faculties as a singer, and these were exerted in low public-houses, where remuneration was generally beer, or halfpence convertible into beer. Her audiences were not fastidious; her songs were not always unobjectionable; and she further became liable to infirmities of temper, and acquired habits of inconvenient violence; became signalised for artful frauds and cunning concealments, and in all respects negligent in her habits. At last she was pronounced to be insane, and found refuge, the only refuge in this world, from worldly misery, in an asylum; but she could scarcely appreciate even the comforts of an asylum. The beds and the clothing might be good, and the food; but the limitation of beer constituted a permanent grievance.

. . . But such lives and even such faces, ought not to pass by us unheeded, like the idle wind, or the clouds of summer. This poor creature knew no instruction. Her ear, possibly attuned to melody, enabled her to pick up the current minstrelsy of the streets, the tunes of organs, and the words of ribald songsters. Moral control there was none; moral examples there were none either. Religious instruction there was none; she had probably never been in a church in her life. So, when life was departing, no aspirations could well arise, nor could the most pious words be expected to prevail. If a feeling remained, or a desire, it was but for the speedier oblivion of more beer. Such results are shocking, and to ears polite scarcely suited; but such results are true.

152

On the Application of Photography to the Physiognomic and Mental Phenomena of Insanity by Dr H.W. Diamond

It would never be expected, a priori, that a new science could arrive at anything like maturity in the space of fifty years, yet with respect to Photography we witness the gratifying fact that the early labours of Wedgwood, Davy and Young, at the commencement of the present century, have been so zealously followed up, that the fundamental difficulties in the theory of this new science have been overcome, and its practical rules very generally established.

That I have been a fellow worker with those who have obtained these valuable results will always be a source of the highest pleasure, and I trust I shall not be looked upon as presenting a premature offering if I venture to lay before the Royal Society a short account of the peculiar application of Photography which my position in the Surrey Asylum has enabled me to make.

The investigation of the Phenomena of Insanity can never be looked upon as a subject of but little interest in a country which has provided so largely for the treatment of Mental Derangement. The Metaphysician and Moralist, the Physician and Physiologist will approach such an enquiry with their peculiar views, definitions and classifications. The Photographer, on the other hand, needs in many cases no aid from any language of his own, but prefers rather to listen, with the picture before him, to the silent but telling language of nature. It is unnecessary for him to use the vague terms which denote a difference in the degree of mental suffering, as for instance, distress, sorrow, deep sorrow, grief, melancholy, anguish, despair; the picture speaks for itself with the most marked precision and indicates the exact point which has been reached in the scale of unhappiness between the first sensation and its utmost height – similarly the modifications of fear, and the more painful passions, anger and rage, jealousy and envy (the frequent concomitants of insanity) being shown from the life by the Photographer, arrest the attention of the thoughtful observer more powerfully than any laboured description.

What words can adequately describe either the peculiar character of the palsy which accompanies sudden terror when without hope, or the face glowing with heat under the excitement of burning anger, or the features shrunk and the skin corrugated and ghastly under the influence of pale rage? Yet the Photographer secures with unerring accuracy the external phenomena of each passion as the really certain indication of internal derangement, and exhibits to the eye the well-known sympathy which exists between the diseased brain and the organs and features of the body.

An Asylum on a large scale supplies instances of delirium with raving fury and spitefulness, or delirium accompanied with an appearance of gaiety and pleasure in some cases, and with constant dejection and despondency in others, or imbecility of all the faculties with a stupid look of general weakness, and the Photographer catches in a moment the permanent cloud, or the passing storm or sunshine of the soul and thus enables the Metaphysician to witness and trace out the connection between the visible and the invisible in one important branch of his researches into the Philosophy of the human mind.

M. Esquirol has described in a striking and accurate manner the aspect of the countenance peculiar to that stage of dementia which is characterized by confirmed incoherence, a chronic Mania (of which I exhibit two illustrative portraits), but those who never witness this exhibition of human suffering, either in the original or in the copy *drawn to the life*, can hardly imagine this peculiar state of mental prostration.

Professor Heinroth gives a graphic description of the Phenomena of raving madness in cases which display the greatest intensity of the disease. In the first stage we witness the forehead contracted, the eyebrows drawn up, the hair bristled and the eyeballs prominent as if pushed out of their orbits. In the second stage nothing can be compared to the truly satanic expression of the countenance, and the Phenomena of the loss of reason in their greatest intensity – and in the third stage the violent paroxysms cease, the countenance is pallid and meagre, and the disease subsides into a permanent fatuity. Photography, as is evident from the portraits which illustrate this paper, confirms and extends this description, and that to such a degree as warrants the conclusion that the permanent records thus furnished are at once the most concise and the most comprehensive.

There is another point of view in which the value of portraits of the Insane is peculiarly marked – viz. in the effect which they produce upon the patients themselves. I have had many opportunities of witnessing this effect. In very many cases they are examined with much pleasure and interest, but more particularly in those which mark the progress and cure of a severe attack of Mental Aberration. I may particularly refer to the four portraits which represent different phases of the case of the same young person commencing with that stage of Mania which is marked by the bristled hair, the wrinkled brow, the fixed unquiet eye, and the lips apart as if from painful respiration, but passing, not to a state in which no man could tame her, but happily through less excited stages to the *perfect* cure. In the third portrait the expression is tranquil and accompanied with the smile of sadness instead of the hideous laugh of frenzy. The hair falls naturally and the forehead alone retains traces, tho' slight ones, of mental agitation. In the fourth there is a perfect calm. The poor maniac is cured.

This patient could scarcely believe that her last portrait, representing her as clothed and in her right mind, could ever have been preceded by anything so fearful; and she will never cease, with these faithful monitors in her hand, to express the most lively feelings of gratitude for a recovery so marked and unexpected. I feel that I shall be supported by the Chaplain to our Asylum if I draw a Moral truth from these portraits, which if I apprehend it rightly amounts to this: that religion can win its way to hearts barred against every other influence, that it can soften and conquer dispositions which would else remain intractable and savage; and that hereby in addition to all its other and higher merits, it establishes a title to be considered the great humanizer of Mankind.

It is of course beside my purpose to allude to the value of Photographic Physiognomy in marking the varied Phenomena of sane Mental Power as exhibited in the different cast of countenance in the Philosopher, the Mathematician, the Poet, the Warrior etc., but I may observe that the study of Physiognomy is equally necessary when tracing the characteristic features of different mental diseases in their commencement, continuance and cure. Nor in a sanitary point of view is it unimportant, for many a time the practised eye of the Physician may see the storm approaching and by remedial and preventive measures can greatly subdue its force.

There are cases, however, in which the most anxious forethought and watchful care are of no avail; and this was the case with the unhappy patient whose small portrait is placed fifth in the frame. It cannot be examined without deep interest and it is thus described by M. Ernest Lacan of Paris: '*La vue s'arrête longtemps sur le portrait d'une femme en proie à la monomanie du suicide. Celle-là, arrivée à la maturité de l'âge, devait être bien belle quand toutes les fraîches illusions souriaient à sa jeunesse. Le malheur est venu, puis la maladie, mais sans pouvoir retirer à ses traits leur beau caractère. Et cependant que de tristesse, que de plaintes, que de déceptions dans ce regard! Que d'inquiétudes, de sombres pensées, de projets sinistres sur ce front plissé! Que de larmes à peine séchées sur ces joues flétries! Que d'amertume, de douleur contenue, de sanglots étouffés, dans cette bouche dont le sourire devait avoir tant de grâce autrefois! . . .*

'*Si l'expression de désespoir, dont ce pâle visage est empreint, n'indiquait pas un dégoût profond de la vie, et* *une pensée sinistre sans cesse présente, la large cicatrice que cette infortunée porte au milieu du cou suffirait pour tout dire. Cette épreuve est tout un drame émouvant.'* [Ernest Lacan, *'La Photographie en Angleterre: Portraits de Folles par le Dr Diamond'*, *La Lumière*, Dec 23 1854.]*

After this description, almost prophetic in its terms, it will scarcely excite surprise if I state that this patient, after many cunning but disappointed attempts, eventually carried out her fatal purpose and Photography has recorded the last page in the fearful drama – of this picture M. Lacan says: *'Cette épreuve donne amplement matière à l'étude et à la réflexion. Le visage de cette femme, contracté pendant la vie, s'est rasséréné dans la mort. Le calme s'est fait sur ces traits naguère agités convulsivement; son oeil entr'ouvert, sa bouche presque souriante semblent exprimer la satisfaction d'un désir assouvi. Est-ce un dernier symptôme de la maladie? Ou bien, la raison étant revenue au moment suprême, est-ce l'expression du sentiment que la malheureuse créature devait éprouver en se voyant délivrée d'une vie de misère et de douleur? C'est à la science qu'il appartient de répondre.'* [Ernest Lacan, *Esquisses Photographiques*, Paris 1856, p. 76.]†

As a contrast to this melancholy story I may refer with pleasure to a case in which Photography unquestionably led to the cure. A.D., aged 20, was admitted under my care in August, 1854, having been recently discharged uncured from the Bethlem Hospital after a year's residence there. Her delusions consisted in the supposed possession of great wealth, and of an exalted station as a Queen. Any occupation was therefore looked upon by her as beneath her dignity. I wished to possess portraits of several patients who imagined themselves to be Queens and Royal Personages, and one of these in a dominant attitude and with a band or 'diadem' round the head, stands first in the frame. It was however not without much persuasion that I induced the Queen, A.D., to give me the honour of a sitting – I told her that it was my wish to take portraits of all the Queens under my care, and I well remember the contempt with which she observed: 'Queens indeed! How did they obtain their titles?' I replied, as she did, *they imagined them* – 'No,' she said sharply, 'I never imagine such foolish delusions, they are to be pitied, but I was born a Queen.' Her subsequent amusement in seeing the portraits and her frequent conversation about them was the first decided step in her gradual improvement, and about four months ago she was discharged perfectly cured, and laughed heartily at her former imaginations.

The illustrative portraits to which I have not specially alluded, viz. the examples of Melancholy, in which even the hands speak the language of sorrow, the type of Epileptic Mania, and some of the smaller portraits, for the most part tell their own tale, with perhaps the exception of the remarkable illustration of Catalepsy as exhibited in the patient who is seated in an armchair with her body erect, the hands raised to the height of the eyes, the arms rigid, and the whole face imprinted with the Characters of Death. In this position or in any other in which she might be placed she would remain motionless and insensible for hours.

The portraits of the Insane are valuable to Superintendents of Asylums for reference in cases of readmission. It is well known that the portraits of those who are congregated in prisons for punishment have often times been of much value in recapturing some who have escaped, or in proving with little expense, and with certainty, a previous conviction; and similarly the portraits of the Insane who are received into Asylums for protection, give the eye so clear a representation of their case that on their

---

* Our attention is caught by a portrait of a woman suffering from suicidal monomania. Of mature years, she must indeed have been beautiful when she was young and innocent. Great unhappiness, and later sickness, have not detracted from her fine features. Yet what anxiety, grave thoughts, and dark intentions show in her expression! So many scarce-dried tears on her withered cheeks! Such bitterness, suppressed sorrow and stifled sobs in that mouth which must once have smiled so sweetly. . . .

If the look of despair on this pale face is not proof of a deep revulsion toward life, and of a continuing ominous cast of thought, the broad scar right across the neck of this poor woman leaves no room for doubt. This picture is a moving experience.

† This print provides ample material for study and reflection. The woman's face, so strained in life, has become serene in death. Calm has spread over those features, formerly tormented by convulsions; her half-open eyes, her almost smiling mouth seem to express the satisfaction of a desire fulfilled. Is this a final symptom of the illness? Or does it rather express what the unfortunate creature must have felt as her reason returned in the supreme moment of deliverance from a life of misery and pain? Only science can give us the answer.

re-admission after temporary absence and cure – I have found the previous portrait of more value in calling to my mind the case and treatment, than any verbal description I may have placed on record.

In conclusion I may observe that Photography gives permanence to these remarkable cases, which are types of classes, and make them observable not only now but for ever, and it presents also a perfect and faithful record, free altogether from the painful caricaturing which so disfigures almost all the published portraits of the Insane as to render them nearly valueless either for purposes of art or of Science.

Wandsworth, April 1856